TEACHING WRITING

TEACHING

WRITING

HOWARD PIERSON

PRENTICE-HALL, INC.

Englewood Cliffs, New Jersey

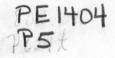

10 9 8 7 6 5 4 3 2 1

P: 0–13–896308–8
C: 0–13–896316–9

Library of Congress Catalog Card Number:
73–37782

Printed in the United States of America

Prentice-Hall International, Inc., *London*
Prentice-Hall of Australia, Pty. Inc., *Sydney*
Prentice-Hall of Canada, Ltd., *Toronto*
Prentice-Hall of India Private Limited, *New Delhi*
Prentice-Hall of Japan, Inc., *Tokyo*

To LAMIE

CONTENTS

PREFACE

In this book which I have written for English teachers in secondary schools and college, particularly junior college, I attempt to provide a convenient and concise statement regarding prevailing tendencies and issues in teaching writing. They are related to correction, the tutorial conference, motivating composition, grammar, research, and lack of nerve among some teachers in the face of electronic cultism. As for electronic cultists, I try to answer them less from a desire to swing Carrie Nation's ax at television sets than from my wish to explain where and why McLuhan errs, and why writing continues to be a useful craft.

Newcomers to English teaching may discover here what others have done to contend with classroom writing problems that all of us encounter. If veterans in the field recognize a kindred spirit, who has lived through many a writing class, and if the cause of teaching competent, even adequate, writing is helped an iota, then I will be most grateful.

ACKNOWLEDGMENTS

The author is indebted to the following professionals and students for their assistance and for their permission to use uncopyrighted materials: Linda Abrams, Robert Antkow, Larry Binenfeld, Marian Brannan, Clifford P. Chabina, Roy Civille, Kathleen Cozzetto, Robert B. Denis, Paul B. Diederich, Albert Eichel, Melvin Fried, Lori Gershen, Debra Greenbaum, Carla Greenberg, Wendy Haft, Nancy Hartner, Robert J. Havighurst, Debra Hochman, Brian Hurley, James A. Hynes, Meryl Insler, Ruth Lovelock, Debra Maake, Carol Morris, David Pike, Jane Schwartz, Lauren Sutherland, Richard Wellington, Edward N. White, and Debra Zayer. Special thanks go to Marcia Lesser, who supplied several examples of student writing and who made the tape of a composition conference.

Thanks also are extended to the owners and/or publishers of copyrighted titles for their permission to reprint selections from the following:

The General Dynamics Editorial Stylebook; 1967, General Dynamics.

High School English Instruction Today, James R. Squire and Roger K. Applebee; 1968, National Council of Teachers of English; Appleton-Century-Crofts, Educational Division, Meredith Corporation, and NCT English.

The American Tradition in Literature, third edition, volume I, "Letter to Dr. Walter Jones," Thomas Jefferson; Sculley Bradley, Richmond Croom Beatty, and E. Hudson Long, editors; 1956, Grosset & Dunlap, Inc.

Assessing Compositions, London Association for the Teaching of English; 1965, LAT English; Blackie and Son, Limited.

Look on Norman Mailer; 1969, Cowles Communications.

The New York Times, 1969/1963, The N.Y. Times Company

New Trends in the Teaching of English in the Secondary Schools, William Evans and Jerry Walker; 1966, Rand McNally and Co.

Poems for Modern Youth, C. L. Edson, "Ravin's of Piute Poet Poe;" Adolph Gillis and William Rose Benet, editors; 1938, Houghton Mifflin Co.

Journal of Educational Research, 1966, "Sequential Patterns of Structures in the English Language," Doctor Frances Miller; Dembar Educational Research Services and Dr. Miller, English Consultant, South Central Educational Unit.

The Teaching of Writing in Our Schools, Richard Corbin; 1966, NCTE; Macmillan Book Company.

Theories of Counseling and Psychotherapy, C. H. Patterson; 1966, Harper & Row Publishers, Inc.

Understanding Media, Marshall McLuhan; 1964, McGraw-Hill Book Company.

California English Journal, 1968, "Peer Correction vs. Teacher Correction of Writing," Howard Pierson, California Association of Teachers of English.

The Roberts English Series/7, Paul Roberts; 1967, Harcourt Brace Jovanovich, Inc.

Howard Pierson

TEACHING
WRITING

WRITING ABANDONED

I

Two attitudes discourage the teaching of writing today. One is that writing is too difficult to teach. The other is that there is no need to learn how to write. Since attitudes are more emotional than intellectual, there is no advantage in refuting them with facts and logic. They will be approached then as matters to be understood or perhaps even as paradoxes to be resolved.

The first attitude immediately gives rise to the paradox that few can write but many write. The second creates the even more fascinating paradox that more and fewer write.

UNRIDDLING SOME RIDDLES ABOUT WRITING

To unriddle the former, one must study its sources, such as articles in professional journals, particularly college English teachers' publications, in which a university professor would typically say that writing is a complicated process that most people can never master.

Now professor!

At one time perhaps few Americans could write anything, but today most can write their own names and addresses, as well as a sentence or two on a post card. Many also can write personal and business letters several paragraphs long and can adequately complete employment applications, questionnaires, and forms for auto licenses, credit cards, etc.

But the English professor must have a more difficult type of writing in mind, when he writes that statement—novels, magazine articles, poems, plays, short stories, essays—all creative efforts requiring talent that is certainly not universal. Or he may be referring to dissertations, theses, and term papers written in colleges. When the professor says that writing is beyond most people, perhaps he means that college students are not writing as well for academic purposes as is expected of them. This explains *few can write*. At the same time, more Americans are writing more frequently and competently than before, because more are attending and completing high school and college than ever before. This explains *many write*.

The paradox that *few can write but many write* may be clarified further by the increase in college enrollments that requires youths to undergo the rigors of college writing. While they are learning, the many related problems frustrate their teachers to such a point that some conclude that writing is much too difficult to teach.

No self-respecting teacher, however, will admit that he feels unable to teach writing; it seems better to have the viewpoint that writing is useless, a sour conclusion similar to the one drawn by the fox who had trouble reaching the grapes. And if this conclusion can be presented as a scholarly finding, so much the better—creating a virtue out of necessity.

Not only does this conclusion assert that there is no need for writing, but it even makes writing appear positively repugnant. Consequently, at a time when Americans are scaling heights of literacy, when paper work inundates offices and households, when publications proliferate and junk mail overbrims the letterbox, restive teachers longen to goon on pilgrimages, to hear oracles emerging from their electrified grottoes and prophesying the imminent doom of writing.

The second paradox is *more and fewer write*. *More write* can be explained by school enrollments; *fewer write* means that writing is on the wane and will soon cease to be a problem—because the electronic revolution is here.

To proclaim that writing is languishing and even dying of a nameable disease—linearity—also is modishly to break with convention. For the first time in scribal history, it is fashionable to deprecate not only inadequate and incompetent writing but all writing.

At the birth of civilization, when the priests of Akkad and Sumer traced in cuneiform wedgemarks the victories of kings, people set great store in writing and deferred to the caste who were privileged to write. The Egyptians, the Hebrews, and the Greeks respected the written word. During the European and Asian middle ages, members of the ruling classes took pride in their ability to play music and to write. As towns and commerce grew and, later, as the factory system developed, writing was regarded as an asset not only by gentlemen but also by tradesmen and proprietors. In nineteenth century America, when the need to Americanize immigrants coincided with the movement to abolish child labor, free public schools were opened for all to learn to read and to write. Writing joined national holiday celebrations as a tradition of schooling and was sung as one of a commonplace trinity—the Rs. But today no Franklin claims that he acquired a graceful written style by imitating sentences in the third volume of *The Spectator*. Nor may one announce that he relies on *The Elements of Style* by William Strunk, Jr. and E. B. White.

McLUHAN ON WRITING

Marshall McLuhan, university teacher and writer has provided the rationale for the desertion of writing and has emerged as a spokesman for those who question the time-honored assumptions about the importance of writing. McLuhan is using social theories that ascribe culture and behavior essentially to developments in communication techniques and is observing in society the growth of electronics and a corresponding atrophy of writing and printing. "The medium, or process, of our time—electric technology—is reshaping and restructuring patterns of social interdependence and every aspect of our personal life."[1]

In McLuhan's view television, films, records, tapes, and the telephone, not books, are man's "extensions" into the world around him. Therefore, talking and listening rather than writing and reading are becoming the prevailing mode of communication as they were before, when men lived in tribes. Since communication media determine peoples' thoughts and feelings, and since reading was the perception of linear elements strung together in a sequence, the print culture "fostered and encouraged a fragmenting process, a process of specialism and detachment"—ordered, structured, patterned, individualized, logical. In other words, reading and writing tended to separate people from one another. In total contrast, the electrical media cause men to perceive, think, and relate in a manner that is characteristically unified, intuitive, involved, simultaneous, collective, integrated, and tribal.

And the new media work these transformations in society not by what they transmit but by how they transmit.

> The medium is the message. This is merely to say that the personal and social consequences of any medium—that is, of any extension of ourselves—result from the new scale that is introduced into our affairs by each extension of ourselves, or by any new technology . . . The instance of the electric light may prove illuminating in this connection. The electric light is pure information. It is a medium without a message, as it were, unless it is used to spell out some verbal ad or name . . . What we are considering here, however, are the psychic and social consequences of the designs or patterns as they amplify or accelerate existing processes. For the "message" of any medium or technology is the change of scale or pace or pattern that it introduces into human affairs . . . Whether the light is being used for brain surgery or night baseball is a matter of indifference . . . it is the medium that shapes and controls the scale and form of human association and action. The content or uses of such media are as diverse as they are ineffectual in shaping the form of human association . . . The message of the electric light is like the message of electric power in industry, totally radical, pervasive, and decentralized. For electric light and power are separate from their uses, yet they eliminate time and space factors in human association exactly as do radio, telegraph, telephone, and TV, creating involvement in depth.[2]

ANSWERS TO McLUHAN

Other students of communication media question, modify, and reject some of the distinctions that McLuhan makes between print and electronic communications. Print, they point out, is not alone in its linearity. Speech sounds or phonemes also are strung together in sequences. If the phonemes of the English word *pot* are scrambled, different meanings are created with the sequences *top* and *opt* and zero meanings with *pto, otp* and *tpo*. Filmed and televised images also are presented in ordered sequences. The television

[1] Marshall McLuhan and Quentin Fiore, *The Medium is the Massage; an Inventory of Effects* (New York: Bantam Books, 1967), p. 8.
[2] Marshall McLuhan, *Understanding Media: The Extensions of Man* (New York: McGraw-Hill, 1964), pp. 7–9.

image itself is linear, consisting of straight lines of bright and dark segments as in a photoengraving. Even electricity as a form of energy is linear to those who conceive of it as streams of electrons flowing through wire lines. Dismissing print as linear is a typical instance of the pot calling the kettle black.

It is also arbitrary to call the effects of electric media intuitive and the effects of print logical, although making such a distinction appeals strongly to those who champion the id in its struggle with the ego. The fact is that both writing and cinematography can be used to convey either emotions or intelligence or both. Now it cannot be denied that a film maker can add image and sound, particularly music, to words in order to enhance feeling. But image and sound may also, by their very concreteness, place limits upon the imagination and upon emotional response that the printed word does not.

> Heard melodies are sweet, but those unheard
> Are sweeter; therefore, ye soft pipes, play on;
> Not to the sensual ear, but, more endeared,
> Pipe to the spirit ditties of no tone.

Neither can it be denied that film and television enable audiences to see and hear people, places, and things that words leave abstract and remote. Because of these media, U.S. Presidents now have personalities and are no longer just names. However, these media in themselves hardly arouse involvement in the sense of commitment or even sympathy. Awareness is not involvement. Nor is involvement a mechanical and conditioned response to sensory stimuli or to their mode of transmission. It is rather a complicated ethical choice and therefore not a simple consequence of electricity. It also is unfortunately true that a particular aspect of American film and television, namely violence, has apparently, through over-exposure, induced in some viewers the opposite of involvement—indifference to human suffering. Such a response is surely tribal but not in the euphemistic sense intended by McLuhan.

The position of some McLuhanists can be found in the bromide that a picture is worth a thousand words. Words are sequential and therefore unable to represent reality, which is composed of simultaneous rather than successive events. This is intended to show that cinematography, being simultaneous, is superior to writing. Such a claim is illusory, however, for photography can no more duplicate the multiplicity of life than can words. Of course, film makers have projected simultaneous images onto screens, but these are no better an approximation of reality than parallel columns of type in newspapers. Even if a way were found to multiply communications infinitely, the effort would be pointless, because viewers, readers, participants, audiences, etc., generally can concentrate on only one image or line of type at one time. Indeed, this concentration is attenuated and lost, when one is exposed to television and films excessively. As Pope Paul VI has observed, "The many images become impressed on the memory and finally on the mind . . . they substitute for thought, fill the mind with vain phantoms, encourage imitation and superficiality."

It is difficult to perpetuate a mystique of simultaneity in electronic communications, whose pantheon numbers only engineers who can send multiple telephone messages over one wire and "electric circus" proprietors, who purvey multiple slide shows and sounds as entertainment.

The most questionable of McLuhan's gospels is that the medium is the message. His critics point out that he appears to accept without reservation certain retrogressive tendencies in modern life, when he hails a new age of electricity, and when he gives no thought to the purposes for which men use the media. Mario Pei, Professor of Romance Philology at Columbia University, voices a legitimate revulsion against sexual and violent sensationalism in films and against "tasteless, graceless, greedy" television commercials.

> By and large man is still a thinking, rational, critical animal, and wants to remain one . . . The linear, reflective, individualistic type of thought betokened by the written, printed word is not dead because we have added an audiovisual dimension.[3]

While McLuhanism has provided a fashionable but rather shaky rationale for those who want writing to disappear, it is not entirely mistaken in directing serious attention to the newer media that are giving school boys and girls an awareness of events their texts and classroom discussions cannot otherwise provide. In addition, closed-circuit television and videotape are being used to teach large groups and to help absentees catch up with missed lessons. Oddly enough, certain aspects of McLuhanism also have been good in suggesting stylistic departures.

MOVIES AS A WRITING MODEL

Some McLuhanists would improve writing by using the cinema as a model. The master himself preaches this idea by precept and example. His foremost is *The Medium is the Massage,* a book of collaboration in tune with his notion of collectivism and full of visuals in the form of microphotographs, distortions, surreals, nudes, news photos, art reproductions, drawings, cartoons, and even blank pages.

There also is a variety of print: headlines, repeated segments, backward and upside down passages, and poetic and prose quotations. Little continuity exists other than through repetition. When not expressing himself through such collage but in publications of more traditional format, McLuhan advocates abandoning story lines for what he calls compressed overlays, presumably to attain the simultaneity that he values. To this end he holds up as a model James Joyce's *Finnegan's Wake,* which meanders like the River Liffey and is full of compressed overlays in the form of portmanteau words and puns. "What can't be coded can be decorded if an ear aye sieze what no eye ere grieved for." Such playfulness with language is attractive to the young, who find it quite iconoclastic in tone. After a stern lecture by an administra-

---

[3]Mario Pei, *What's in a Word; Language—Yesterday, Today, and Tomorrow* (New York: Hawthorn Books, 1968), p. 157.

tor on the need for teachers to discipline students *in loco parentis,* a young teacher wrote the following graffito on a blackboard: "in low-kiss pry-wrentis." McLuhan also suggests that writers use sudden zooms and cuts as well as elliptical prose for readers conditioned by television advertisements.

Discontinuity can be considered a school of writing today, because its practitioners are becoming numerous. However, discontinuous writing can be found as early as the sixteenth century in *Gargantua and Pantagruel* and the eighteenth century in *Tristram Shandy's* disordered chapters, digressions, and a blank page for the reader to compose his own description of Widow Wadman. Today exponents include Pynchon, Barthelme, and Vonnegut. Thomas Pynchon's novel *V* violates historical time lines and Donald Barthelme imitates Joyce in *City Life* stories. And the works of Kurt Vonnegut are described by a young admirer as follows:

> He writes cinematically—charting themes through time, literarizing jump-cut techniques and split-screen effects. Writers under thirty may be a different breed because their most powerful images are cinematic—that's what they grew up with . . . It's a rare young writer who doesn't know that he's more consistently moved by what he sees on the screen than what he reads. But at the same time the single most powerful communication experience he's had is literary, so he may try, somehow, to wed literary and cinematic into one.[4]

Yet the new style can be abused, as James Kunen, young author of *The Strawberry Statement,* discerns when he says, "If you're under thirty now, anything gets snapped up as a message of one generation to another. You somehow have a license not to organize, not to work out a strict coherency, to splatter yourself across the paper."[5]

Some of the youthful experimenters are not alone; a few members of the English teaching profession also find themselves inhibited by considerations of precision, coherence, and order in writing. Prevalent today is the suggestion that teachers must evaluate the overall effect of a student's theme rather than its organization and clarity. However, the overall effect of writing is largely determined by organization and clarity, as is the overall effect of speech and film. Continuity and coherence are necessary in all communications because the transmission of an idea or picture from sender to receiver becomes garbled and misunderstood without them. According to communication or information theory developed by telephone and telegraph engineers, all language must have a certain amount of redundancy or lack of randomness to be operative. The only way to decode a message in a given language is to study the probability of occurrence of the message's elements in accordance with the structural rules of the language. In addition, structure is needed to compensate for noise or interference, such as an extraneous sound in speech or a misspelled word in writing.

An illustration of this process can be seen in the English nonsentence

---

[4]Craig Karpel, quoted in an interview by Bernard Weinraub, "Young Writers Say They Don't Read," *The New York Times,* May 23, 1969, p. 36.
[5]*Loc. cit.*

"Let's bake a take." We can say that it is highly probable that the writer meant "Let's bake a cake," because *take* does not pattern properly or meaningfully in the position it occupies in the sentence, and because *c* preceding *ake* makes an English word which does pattern correctly. If all of the other letters in the alphabet and in any order could be substituted for *take*, there could be no effective decoding of the message. Therefore, although writing innovators may digress, zoom, and cut, they still cannot press beyond the borderline of coherence without losing their message.

Iconoclasts will also be disappointed to learn that cinema itself is not a total departure from writing but in large measure is derivative. Photographers, screenwriters, and television writers use methods developed by the print culture. For example, both commercial and art photographers respect the idea of sequence, including the causal sequence that McLuhan deprecates, and concern themselves with what they call photographic statements, which typically consist of pictures arranged in a meaningful order. A common sequence is the chronological. Photo one: A man's foot poised above a banana peel. Photo two: Man taking a pratfall. This is a simple cause-and-effect sequence. Another is the pseudochronological, which creates the same effect as the chronological by using photos that actually are unconnected. Such would be the case if the two photos mentioned were of different people or if photo two had been made before photo one. The meaning still depends on the sequence. This truth is also illustrated by changing the order of the photos: If the pratfall precedes the banana peel, the message is not as immediately clear, if clear at all.

Coming to their vocations with experience in writing novels, articles, and radio scripts, screen and television writers know that no film or broadcast is possible without a written script. They also work with technical elements which originated in literature and that enable them to fashion documents that guide all those concerned, such as directors, actors, set designers, and cameramen. The English teacher advises his student to write an introduction to his paper that will attract the reader's attention. Catch the dial wanderer by writing a dramatic preview of the show to go on before the first commercial, the television producer instructs the script writer.

Other items common to both published and filmed fiction include: plot development with conflict, climax, and denouement; theme, characterization, setting, dialogue, and narration. Film theorists sometimes refer to the cuts between shots and the dissolves between scenes, both used as transitions, in terms of the grammar or syntax of film.

To teach movie-making the Eastman Kodak Company has issued a series of films called *Rhetoric of the Movie* with reel titles which include "A Simple Movie Sentence," "Varying the Point of View," and "A Movie Paragraph."

Films also have adopted from literature the tropes of metaphor, symbolism, and irony. In the last scene of *Viva Zapata* the horse is all that is left of Zapata. Ma Joad burns mementoes of a happier life before the family leaves for California in *The Grapes of Wrath*. A hooded monk is a metaphor for death in *The Seventh Seal*. An ardent McLuhanist would be unnerved to read of the noted Russian film maker Eisenstein's claim that Dickens inspired D. W.

Griffith's invention of the superimposed shot, the dissolve, the closeup, and the pan.[6]

Given the dependence of films on writing, one may not be surprised at the fact that, in a typical year of production, American film companies issued 141 movies that originated in published novels, stories, and nonfiction compared to ninety-one titles based on original screen plays.[7] If a novel maintains its popularity, it usually will become a film, as did *Grapes of Wrath*, *Good Earth*, *Arrowsmith*, and *Ulysses*. The public interest aroused by a best seller is often parlayed into a film, which in turn stimulates sales of the novel.

Because of the frequency with which novels become films, people have become used to the association, which is reinforced constantly by reviewers. The literary critic who wishes to convey a certain crassness in a new novel may suggest that the author probably wrote it to attract the attention of a movie producer. The film critic who is disappointed with a movie may lament its inferiority to the novel. He may, on the other hand, comment that it surpasses the novel. Many a social gathering is enlivened by the opportunity to compare novels and films, those participants who have read the novels enjoying a somewhat superior status to the moviegoers.

By employing writers, the movies reveal a need for writing rather than an obsolescence. In some cases, screenplays are written collectively rather than individually. On occasion, a script moves through the hands of as many as six writers between the original outline and the polished end-product, before the producer and director are satisfied. When writers adapt a book for filming, they usually supply what it lacks in dialogue, scenic elements, and action. The personalities and needs of the stars also require modifications of the original. A measure of the writing and revision needed to transform book to film is suggested by the fact that playwright Robert Bolt, author of *A Man for All Seasons*, took fourteen months to write the screenplay of *Lawrence of Arabia*, drawing upon several biographical sources.

Writing, then, is fundamental to the new media, and film and television merely suggest departures in writing style. Thus, teachers of English need not desert writing instruction. Rather they should encourage students to experiment with cinematic techniques in composition, remaining aware, of course, that form is no substitute for ideas. Teachers may also find that classroom photography and movie-making are helpful in stimulating the desire to write, because students enjoy gadgetry and instant visual products; accept the need for captions and commentaries to accompany photographs; and relish composing, producing, and enacting film stories.

SUMMARY

It is one thing to note the influence of electric media in society and another to make a cult of the vacuum tube. Electric power has made notable

---

[6]Quoted by George Bluestone in *Novels into Film* (Berkeley: University of California Press, 1961), p. 2.
[7]Theodore Taylor, *People Who Make Movies* (Garden City: Doubleday and Company, 1967), p. 29.

changes in industrial technology, communications, education, and recreation. But it is not completely accurate that the new media are transforming people to replace logical thought with intuition, independence with involvement, and reading and writing with watching and listening. That thought persists, that the newer media depend on reading and writing, and that print lives on are very evident.

Teachers of English cannot evade their composition teaching responsibilities by using McLuhan to suggest that writing is useless. Rather they must wrestle with the difficulties inherent in teaching and learning to write. In so doing they can proceed to explode the paradoxes by changing *few can write but many write* to *many write and can learn to write better* and by amending *more and fewer write* to *more and more need to write*.

THE USES OF WRITING

II

It may be said of the demise of writing that, like a once premature report of Mark Twain's death, it is greatly exaggerated. Such a statement is, furthermore, inappropriate because it suggests that the predictions of doom are valid although hasty. It would be more truthful to say that writing is indestructible while it continues to serve as a useful medium in communicating ideas and in expressing emotions and while it grows more important as society becomes more complex and as people need more education to perform in the economy.

WRITING AND THINKING

The capacity to facilitate thought is one of the most important benefits of writing. This truth is verified in the experience of teachers, psychologists, and professional writers. In the classroom, not only subjective judgments of instructors but also experimental research has discovered that language study, including writing, can improve the inductive and critical thinking of students.[1] In some investigations, proficiency in writing of elementary and secondary pupils has been significantly associated with intelligence and the ability to reason verbally.[2] Admittedly, this relationship may mean that intelligence causes writing competence or that both are caused by a third variable; it may also signify that writing enhances intelligence. Psychologists, too, have learned from clinical studies that certain language processes are useful in reducing mental disorders. Some point out that neurotic persons are unaware of their inappropriate responses to situations because they have not identified and labeled these responses. The therapists believe that a neurotic can apply reason to his problems if he can acquire words and sentences that correspond to his internal and external experiences.[3] Practice in writing is a means of acquiring these essentials.

[1]David H. Russell, "Higher Mental Processes," *Encyclopedia of Educational Research,* third edition, p. 657.
[2]Walter D. Loban, *The Language of Elementary School Children* (Champaign, Ill.: NCTE, 1963), p. 87; Nathan S. Blount, "The Effect of a Study of Grammar on the Writing of Eighth-Grade Students," ERIC Report No. ED 036515 (Madison: Wisconsin University Research and Development Center for Cognitive Learning, 1968).
[3]C. H. Patterson, *Theories of Counseling and Psychotherapy* (New York: Harper and Row, 1966), p. 192.

10

Even normal intelligence depends on the ability to perceive relationships and to apply reason to solve problems. To perceive connections one must be able to discern similarities and differences among the objects and the processes that he observes. Writing sharpens and deepens perception because its practitioner must employ language with rigor and discrimination. Each noun or verb, for example, that a writer chooses is an expression of a similarity and a difference, a genus and a species. The genus of a word is the category to which its referent, the thing labeled, belongs. The species of a word serves as a means of separating and discriminating among referents of the same genus. Thus the verb *walk* pertains to a genus of words that express motion on foot and include similar words like *skip, jump,* and *run.* The species of *walk* is the fact that it denotes the kind of motion on foot that occurs at a moderate and continuous pace as distinguished from other kinds of paces implied by other word members of the genus. Writers can discriminate between experiences not only by carefully selecting words that express nuances or differences but also by qualifying words with other words, such as nouns and verbs with adjectives and adverbs. Not to be able to find similarities or to qualify differences is to think vaguely and inexactly. Francis Bacon spoke truly when he said that writing makes an exact man.

To solve problems intelligently one has to impart sense and order to experience. Not only must he pattern the materials of his perceptions according to similarities and differences but also with reference to more complex relationships, such as cause and effect, coordination and subordination, location in place and time, and induction and deduction. Language enables writers to organize such relationships by means of prepositions and conjunctions (*before, because*), syntax (*John fed Mary, Mary fed John*), transitional adverbs (*also, too*) and sequences of paragraphs.

"The only way I can figure out what I really think about anything is to write about it," notes Norman Mailer.[4] His comment implies that writing can help considerably to assess the worth of his own ideas. This is true even of the nonprofessional writer.

A college student recently wrote a letter to the editor of a local newspaper, expressing disagreement with consumer advocate Ralph Nader's criticisms of the unsafe features of a certain auto. The writer began with a strong assertion that Nader was wrong. Next came sentences refuting each of Nader's specific claims. Then, the student drafted his conclusion, which was that perhaps the auto was not as good as it should have been. When asked to explain his unexpected ending, he revealed that, as he tried to rebut each of Nader's charges, he found himself unable to provide a factual and persuasive counterargument. By the time he finished his letter, he realized that his original opinion had been emotionally and poorly reasoned. The process had clarified his thoughts.

Writing also helps people to retain thought. There is a scene in a Chaplin film in which Charlie has a job as a singing waiter. Typically unprepared for his new vocation, he writes the words to his song on his detachable shirt

---

[4]Quoted in *Look*, May 27, 1969, p. 28.

cuffs. When he appears for his big number, the cuffs enable him to sing with abandon, so much so that, as he gesticulates to the audience, throwing his arms open in the manner of a tenor who is reaching the high note of his aria, he shoots his cuffs off and thereby loses his prompts, creating another predicament for the little tramp. Writing is an irreplaceable aid to memory, used by public speakers, housewives, office workers, and business personnel. Men in public office ready their comments on notecards or read aloud from speeches already written out in full, especially if the matter is such that it may be quoted by critics or cited in the press for all to read and judge. Housewives post reminders on wall calendars and kitchen bulletin boards, and their husbands use date books and desk organizers. The vocation of stenography thrives upon the usefulness of written notes.

It is true that tape recorders are assuming some of the functions of written memory aids, performing such services as taking dictation and preserving public voices and events for history. However, there are still certain advantages in written transcription. One can read written materials more quickly and more accurately, as the persistence of court reporting testifies. Sound recording is not as exact as writing, because many differently spelled words and phrases sound alike; e.g., She made a mistake, She made him a steak; heedless, he'd less; infective, invective; bitter, bidder; affect, effect, and other homonymns.

Some of McLuhan's followers point out that he does not write his books but dictates them into a tape recorder. This is making a very fine distinction between writing and recording. What may be more important is to note that a book dictated on tape must be transcribed into some written form in order to be edited, proofread, and, above all, duplicated. To my knowledge, McLuhan has not yet confined his books to commercial recordings; rather, they are printed books. Imagine trying to skim through a recording of McLuhan's *Understanding Media,* in order to find a quotation.

Other widespread uses of written notes are in professional conferences and in school and college courses, not only in the role of speaker or lecturer but also as audience member or student. The student can train his powers of extended recall by writing an item repeatedly from memory until it is mastered. In addition to helping in preparation for semester examinations, this procedure enables learners to remember the main ideas and many details of complete volumes in training for such professions as law and medicine, which require large accumulations of information.

WRITING AND FEELING

Writing is as serviceable in the expression of emotion as it is in the clarification and the retention of thought. It can be a relief for frustration and rage, a means of developing emotional maturity and sensibility, and a source of feelings of accomplishment in the employment of leisure time.

The employee who must suppress his resentment towards colleagues or superiors sometimes gives vent to his feelings by hammering nails, shouting at his family, or having a few cocktails before dinner. Women who tire of office or household routines may treat themselves to rich desserts or shopping excursions. Any of these discontented persons may find relief in writing a letter. There are employees who, when circumvented, sit down and compose a letter of rebuttal and self-justification that may even extend to sarcasm and denunciation or notice of resignation. Often, after the effort of composition has absorbed wrathful energies and has satisfied his desire to retaliate for his discomforts, the writer lays his letter aside for later disposition. Then, as other events engage his nervous system, he finds himself able to see his original source of irritation in a newer and more rational perspective and discards his letter. Some people get reassurance and support from writing and mailing a letter to a sympathetic friend or relative. Of course, airing one's grievances to a willing listener on the phone serves the same purpose; however, speaking on the phone is not nearly as private and not always as available. People who are lonely and far from home, as soldiers on duty often are, find much solace in writing to intimate acquaintances. To cite these common instances seems to belabor the obvious; yet they constitute irrefutable evidence that there is a popular need for writing.

Letter writing as a social phenomenon is on the increase as a consequence of improved education and because of the greater intensity of interest in public issues. As governmental units and private organizations have assumed the status of forces for control and change, people have turned to them for solutions to problems of war, crime, taxation, consumership, and health. Writing to public officials and to the press is now accepted widely. Such a practice is encouraged by legislators and officeholders who give careful recognition to original letter-writers in the belief that they are probably active voters. Local newspapers publish letters to encourage concern for issues, to sell papers with the appeal of controversy, and to maintain circulation by personalizing their contents. Writing letters of complaint and contention is a useful safety valve for discouragement and resentment that is permitted even in countries with authoritarian regimes.

STUDENT UNREST AND WRITING

Writing has figured largely in the movement of student revolt as a means of expressing indignation against war and authority. Young rebels circulate pamphlets and newspapers on campuses and near military bases. High school boys and girls issue underground journals in defiance of administrators. Their authors and readers consider such publications as a means of transmitting the youth culture. They are written in a jargon that provides a sense of community and exclusiveness and that is laced heavily with curse words, neologisms like *groove* and *grok*, and revolutionary catchphrases, such as "Up against the wall."

Twenty-nine students at the Lawrence, New York, High School used more conventional language when they wrote an eighty-page critique of their school. Their report expressed feelings about race relations, curriculum, guidance services, and teaching. About their literature studies in English classes, they held the opinion that

. . . literature has become a study in quantity rather than quality. The result is a superficial understanding and little appreciation. When 40 poems are covered it becomes a game in which author, title, and main ideas are memorized for testing purposes. The analysis of novels and plays too often becomes an unnecessary plot summary. The student must be taught to critically dissect these works.[5]

The contribution of such writing to the improvement of education is debatable; it may be that there are students who at least can detect when something is wrong with how, if not what they are learning. Less moot, however, is the fact that a number of Lawrence youths utilized the written word to give vent to strong emotions.

The dependence of young persons on writing is not a recent outgrowth of student unrest. Adolescence has long been a period when rapid physiological changes and emancipation from parental supervision give rise to uncertainty, bewilderment, and anxiety about one's identity and competency. It is a time of introspection, when a youth not only searches his features in the mirror but also records his feelings in a diary by writing secret verse and stories in which fantasies realize ambitions in heroic or tragic deeds; he also sends letters to friends and pen pals who seem to understand his preoccupations more than does his family. His reluctance to compose essays for school assignments is perhaps equaled by his zeal in passing notes to his classmates. The volume of such correspondence is quite large, judging from evidences left on classroom floors and in school corridors. The interested gleaner of such discarded notes sees messages about encounters with members of the opposite sex, arrangements for meetings and excursions, schoolwork and tests, frictions with peers and adults, and the boredom and excitement of going through a school day.

A particularly faithful correspondent, one young man writes to a girl: "Well, since I'm writing you when you owe me a note, you better write me a good one. This one is pretty long." Another conscientious note-passer, Claudia by name, writes to a friend, Marge, "Hi, how's life? Mrs. S. didn't collect the homework today because she is going to collect it tomorrow. Today's homework is pages 330–331, even exercises 4–10. Do it. I hope that boy Ralph is cute."

Sometimes life is frustrating because it is rich. A young woman named Chris sends a message to her friend Merrill: "I am writing you to say I hope you had a wonderful trip. How was it? I was mad today. I had my money in for the trip, too. But since I have to play at the concert tomorrow night I asked Mr. K. if I could go. He said I shouldn't, so I got my money back."

Enjoyment of the new media finds expression in writing. To a schoolmate Ginnie, Laurie writes, "Hi ya? How are you? Guess what I'm doing now besides writing you. I'm listening to the play version of West Side Story in stereo. It's soooooo different. They sing different and some of the words are different. 'America' is on. Ooh, it's got different words."

Occasionally, the young write to drive away boredom. Donna scribbles this to Sue: "I'm in social studies, and we are doing nothing. I just finished

[5]Lawrence, New York, students critique, 1969, p. 17.

my science homework and I have time left so I am writing you a note. P.S. Write back." Once in a while, despite the press of classwork, a personal matter demands a note: "In English class she wrote me a note and said something about you. She said I shouldn't tell you, but if you wanna know I'll tell you in my next letter, OK? You are definitely walking to my locker with me. Make her go alone." Confessions can temporarily supersede mathematics. "For about two months people kept telling me that you had changed for the worst. Some of them I believed, most I did not. When I was with you about a month ago, I found out you didn't. I'm sorry for even thinking that of you. Forgive me? Susan still doesn't want me being with you but if she can I can."

Because adolescence is a time when boy meets girl, notes celebrate the matter in various ways. "The boy that Linda likes is coming to the party and is going to fight Greg. Greg is going to have a problem. He likes Barbara and is taking Linda out. Come over tonight and we will play horseshoes." Richard sends the following comment to Mary-Ann: "Look, I know this is know way to ask you but, Would you go Steady With me? I'd write more but I want to see what you say first." And when it comes to difficulties, one finds a friend's advice helpful: "Shelley, What if Steven thinks I like David and David thinks I like him? What should I do? Ann."

Personal writing helps youngsters to understand as well as to express and to relieve their feelings, many teachers believe. They claim that greater maturity and wiser judgment come from such understanding. Such teachers like to give writing assignments that encourage their pupils to perceive the world in original ways and to communicate their observations in language that evokes for the writer and the reader the smell and taste of experience.

Because impersonal writing is emphasized in American secondary schools, teachers here may benefit from the study of examples provided by their British counterparts in fostering creative writing. The compositions of British students are often very sensitive, descriptive, and suggestive of a zest for language. The following is from a composition by an English secondary student named Pamela, who imagines herself as an old woman:

> All I hear all day is tick-tock of the clock, the fire crackling and, noise. The room so dim doesnt seem like the sun wants to come in. It was like this in the old days, although, it seemed cheerful with the children running about. Sometimes the noise seems powerful, old Tom scratching, the clock ticking, fire crackling, his trumpet, boys shouting, banging, kicking, jumping, still makes it seem as Im not alone in my old days.[6]

Some British teachers say that personal writing comes easily to boys and girls and that it inspires them with a desire to write well, a feeling that they do not share when asked to write about impersonal matters. These teachers further believe that students carry over to factual and reportorial assignments many technical skills learned when writing imaginatively.

[6]London Association for the Teaching of English, *Assessing Compositions* (London: Blackie and Son, Limited, 1965), p. 38.

LEISURE-TIME WRITING

As leisure time increases, personal and creative written expression takes on importance in the lives of adults as well as youths. It has been estimated that time away from work has multiplied twenty times since 1930. In addition, people live longer and have longer periods of retirement. Although many citizens waste the bonus of leisure on television, which leaves them feeling restless and unfulfilled, some find satisfactions in writing, and many more would do so if encouraged. Correspondence schools of writing are thriving financially. Community organizations for senior citizens issue publications of verse and prose written by members. To better meet the need for good use of leisure time by all adults Robert J. Havighurst[7] has proposed that communities organize agencies to teach the use of leisure time. Such agencies could help people to obtain a sense of personal accomplishment through imaginative writing, music, art, drama, handicrafts, and other avenues of expression.

Rather than burying reading and writing as fossils, modern technology has made them easier and more accessible. By reducing the hours needed for factory and household labor, technology has further freed men to express themselves in a number of ways, among them writing. In addition, changes in the economy have made society more dependent on writing.

WRITING AND JOBS

A primary aim of schooling is to prepare young people for gainful employment in the nation's economic processes. Many jobs require writing competencies and will demand even more in the predictable future. For what kinds of jobs must education train youth during the present decade? According to projections[8] of labor analysts, there will be little need to prepare farmers, laborers, and semiskilled workers, but there will be much demand in sales, skilled labor, management, clerical, service, and professional and technical fields. Listed in order of increasing growth, the foregoing categories will expand between 21 percent and 45 percent in numbers of personnel.

Because of the increasing complexity of such vocations, their educational requirements will rise considerably during the 1970s, above the level of the 1960s, when in all but service and skilled occupations, training beyond high school was already imperative. Increasingly, the ticket of admission to such jobs is going to be a college diploma. In 1966, students earned 536,000 bachelors degrees, 126,000 masters, and 17,500 doctorates. By 1975, it is expected that degree-granting institutions will issue annually 894,000 bachelors, 220,000 masters, and 35,000 doctorates. To obtain these diplomas, undergraduates and graduates will need to write tens of thousands of term reports, final examination essays, and theses.

[7]Robert J. Havighurst, "The Esthetic Society," unpublished speech at the Conference on the Arts and the Small Community, Wisconsin Idea Theater, Spring Green, Wisconsin, June 29, 1967.

[8]U.S. Bureau of Labor Statistics, *Occupational Outlook Handbook*, Bulletin No. 1550 (Washington, D.C.: U.S. Government Printing Office, 1968), passim.

Besides writing to advance through college, graduates also will need writing skills in many, if not most, of the vocations that they will enter. For example, there probably will be 400,000 more teaching jobs due to growth and 1,500,000 due to replacements. Those who take these posts will have to develop teaching materials, to plan lessons, to write correspondence, and to submit reports. Some also will write for publications.

A traditional view of the importance of writing to teaching is illustrated by a recent controversy that occurred between a local community board of education and a central officer in New York City. The local board requested that license examinations be abolished in the City in order to give the board greater discretion in hiring teachers. Dr. Jay E. Greene reportedly objected because of what might occur if the Board of Examiners, of which he is chairman, no longer screened teachers for clear and correct writing. He cited the following response to an examination question by a candidate: "In presenting their project, the teacher is able to focus more attention on each child individually periodically. The teacher should plan a trip around each project chosen and presented by the group."[9]

Writing also will be valuable in scientific and engineering jobs, which will probably increase faster than most others. Biological scientists with Ph.D.s will be needed for the growing research in heart disease, cancer, and birth defects. At present 40 percent of such personnel are employed in research and development, 25 percent are in management and administration, and others are in writing, consulting, and inspecting. In conducting research, scientists must keep written records of their procedures and findings and must prepare reports of the results of their tests and experiments. Besides biologists, other scientific personnel needed for research, teaching, management, and quality control, all requiring writing, are physicists, mathematicians, geologists, and chemists.

During the 1970s engineering may continue to be a very large employer of professional men and in industries as diverse as aerospace and defense, business machines, chemicals, construction, electronics, machinery, petroleum, and utilities. Here, too, there will be a need for men with advanced degrees to carry out research, development, and teaching. Engineers who design and develop new products, issue reports of inspections and quality controls, and handle administration and management will require writing skills.

Other writing opportunities for engineers will occur in the realms of industrial advertising, public relations, and publication of house organs and business journals. As distinguished from consumer advertising, industrial advertising is a business that conducts marketing communications between industrial corporations. For example, a chemical manufacturer uses industrial advertising to inform a paper mill about his chemical products that are useful in papermaking. The writer of industrial advertising copy also prepares promotional brochures, sales manuals, and catalogs for direct mailing. In addition, he writes scripts for industrial films, scenarios for film strips, and titles

---

[9]*New York Times*, February 6, 1969, p. 36.

and captions for still photographs. Engineers are in demand for such work because they are able to define technical matters precisely and because they speak the same language as engineers who make purchasing decisions. Where there are already 3,000 trade journals circulating among 50,000 business concerns, opportunities for persons who combine technical knowledge with writing ability will continue to abound.

Technical writing is a matter of significance to such firms as Hamilton Standard, Windsor Locks, Connecticut. According to Richard Wellington, professional and scientific recruiting officer:

> At Hamilton Standard we feel that the ability to write well is imperative in order to qualify for many of our technical and professional positions . . . Our product line is of a very technical nature and a good deal of our sales effort is done with the use of formal written proposals. These proposals are prepared by the engineering personnel associated with a specific product line and consequently our sales effectiveness depends upon their writing ability. Also, since the technical products of our modern times have become so sophisticated, it becomes required that considerable written instructions and operation guides must accompany the hardware in order for the customer to effectively install and use the product. Therefore, it is quite evident that writing skill is a very important attribute for an employee.[10]

In certain instances, writing ability is preferred to engineering competency. Robert B. Denis, in charge of management systems at the Quincy, Massachusetts, division of General Dynamics, states that systems and procedures work requires writing skill first and knowledge of a science second. In his opinion, it is easier for an able writer to overcome deficiencies in applied science than for a technician to correct weakness in writing.[11]

Besides making writing competence a condition of employment for technical and professional personnel, General Dynamics tries to improve writing in service by means of house publications and manuals, such as its *ABC of Clear Writing* and *General Dynamics Editorial Stylebook*. *ABC* advises employees ways of composing material that is easy and interesting to read.[12] It includes suggestions for getting to the point quickly, keeping sentences short and simple, using active verbs, and adjusting language to one's readers. Regarding the latter, the booklet advises the use of words that can be understood by colleagues with eleven or twelve years of schooling; specific recommendations are given for controlling the lengths of words and sentences. The stylebook lists prescriptions for usage, capitalizing, spelling, plurals, abbreviations, photo captions, punctuation, and diction. (*"Moisturize.* Despite Madison Avenue's efforts, no dictionary recognizes this as a legitimate word. Use instead *moisten* or *dampen.*")[13]

The Bureau of Labor Statistics predicts that jobs for paraprofessional technicians will increase in number even faster than jobs for the engineers and scientists who will need their help. Such technicians' occupations in-

---

[10]Letter to the author, February 6, 1969.
[11]Letter to the author, February 18, 1969.
[12]General Dynamics, *The ABC of Clear Writing*, Fort Worth, Texas, 1954.
[13]General Dynamics, *Editorial Stylebook*, Ft. Worth, Texas, 1967, p. 34.

clude junior engineers, technical writers, quality control specialists, production and time-study analysts, tool designers, materials testers, and laboratory assistants. Because many of these positions entail the analysis and solution of scientific problems, these workers, too, must write reports.

Health work will probably expand during the 1970s, as a result of population growth, more public concern about health, increased private and public medical coverage, and research in medicine. Biological scientists, physicians, pharmacists, optometrists, speech pathologists, and veterinarians will not only provide direct services to patients but will also teach, conduct research, write for professional journals, and present monographs at meetings. Paramedical workers will increase in number between 30 percent and 100 percent by 1975. Besides having to write during training after high school, such personnel must write at work. Dental hygienists report their inspection findings to parents of school children. Medical record librarians keep, analyze, and summarize records of illnesses and treatments. Occupational therapists rehabilitate the lost writing abilities of disabled persons. Nurses evaluate and record patients' symptoms, and some write lesson plans for teaching nurses' aides and student nurses. Health inspectors report on public, commercial, or industrial health conditions. And supervisors of many kinds of medical personnel assess clinical performance, in writing.

In other growing occupations, such as accounting, market research, and personnel work, the practice of writing will continue. Accountants issue profit and loss statements, cost studies, tax reports, evaluation of financial statements, and dispatches used by industrial managers to make business decisions. Market researchers conduct studies whose recommendations influence commercial sales and consumption. Personnel workers investigate personnel relations, write job descriptions, and compose statements and correspondence with reference to recruitment, labor negotiations, and employees' benefits.

As the trend continues from small and independent companies to large business organizations, managerial occupations, which employed 7,000,000 persons in 1965, probably will have 8,750,000 by 1975. Companies will hire graduates with degrees in business administration as salaried managers in advertising, banking, hotel and restaurant administration, contract administration, payroll management, industrial purchasing, and industrial traffic control. These managers will need to compose memoranda, correspondence, reports, proposals, and assessments of personnel.

Focusing on the duties of a contract administrator reveals a need for very specific writing knowledge. In order to avert differences of interpretation during a contract's performance, he must render agreements of the contracting parties in exact and unambiguous language. Similar requirements exist in the duties of negotiators for labor and management, with the market for such skills enlarging as legislatures pass laws giving public employees the right to bargain collectively.

The trend to larger business organization gives rise not only to more management jobs but also to more written communications. A small firm can make do with informal and spoken procedures for administering salary records and payments. However, a large corporation with branch offices and production centers located far from headquarters must rely on written systems that can be understood clearly and administered uniformly by local managers.[14]

Other vocations that demand competence in writing, which are expected to enlarge during the present decade, are guidance counseling, social work, library service, and religious professions. In addition, clerical occupations, which employed about 11,000,000 persons, mainly women, in 1965, will grow to nearly 14,300,000 by 1975. Although office machine and computer operators will multiply the most, because of technological changes, many more persons also will undertake more traditional kinds of work entailing correspondence and written records, such as typists, secretaries, stenographers, and bookkeepers. These workers will continue to need preparation in spelling, punctuation, usage, vocabulary, and taking notes. Secretaries who are capable of correcting their employers' letters and of composing persuasive and accurate correspondence and memoranda will continue to be in great demand.

Barring catastrophe, there is clearly an economic future for writing competencies in professional, technical, managerial, and clerical occupations, which labor statisticians forecast will employ over 36,000,000 persons by 1975. What can teachers of English do to help prepare these workers for their writing tasks during the 1970s? One measure would be to consult employers and personnel already associated with these occupations. Recently, a small sampling of opinion among employers in hotel management, publishing, petroleum, aviation, business machines, and optics showed a remarkable consistency regarding what schools might provide as writing training for jobs. These executives said that students should learn spelling, grammar, vocabulary, and ways of writing clearly and simply. One corporation vice president urged that teachers afford students practice in writing with word limitation because he finds that the present volume of paper work is so large that employers want correspondents who can express in a half page what others take four pages to say.

An optical firm manager suggested teaching how the nuances of meaning depend on a word's context. He also proposed that students be required to review each other's written efforts. (See section on peer correction, Chapter 3.) According to a supervisor of engineers, secretarial training should not only include courses in correspondence but in writing reports as well. Future engineers, he thinks, should learn how to write technical reports and ways of collecting, editing, and graphically presenting data.

SUMMARY

To summarize, there are many urgent reasons to teach written composition despite tendencies to abandon writing as a formal course of study. Although teaching literature is more fun, although students resist the effort of

---

[14]Letter to the author, by James A. Hynes, Director of Training and Development, Sonesta Hotels, Boston, February 28, 1969.

composing paragraphs of considered ideas, although the mystique of electricity preaches that writing is going the way of quills and inkwells, and although publicists exhort teachers to be "relevant," writing is no less beneficial to thought, no less instrumental to expressing feeling, and no less essential in the workshops of society than it has ever been.

If teachers must continue to teach writing, then how can the problems and resistances be overcome? Is there a best method of teaching composition? Is the conventional way adequate? What alternatives are there? What can be done that is not being done? Has the new linguistics made any change in writing? Is research producing answers?

The chapters that follow describe and assess contemporary influences and resources in the teaching of writing.

CORRECTION FOREVER ?

III

If teachers of English agree on any issue at all, it is that correcting papers is basic to teaching writing. In fact, for many teaching writing means the same thing as correcting papers. Although they may differ in such aspects as: the number of themes assigned; what is accepted as good style and appropriate usage; whether to stress exposition or imagination; giving single or multiple grades; a composition's desired length and what is correct—they nevertheless correct.

Those who know him can readily visualize the typically conscientious English composition teacher. He comes into focus shuffling through his students' manuscripts in the teachers' lounge, in the lunchroom, or perhaps in the assembly hall, as the lights come on, red pencil in hand. Then he reappears with reddening eyes at the dinner table with his wife and children standing near, shaking their heads sympathetically and murmuring, "Daddy is marking his compositions." Come strike or sit-in, wrack or ruin, war or peace, there are always papers to correct.

There are reasons why Daddy corrects. It is a tradition. When he was a schoolboy, his teachers red-penciled his essays. Later, as a cadet-teacher, he was elated by his senior teacher's permission to take home a set of themes; an initiate at last, he corrected papers, just like a real teacher. When Daddy found unthinkable errors, he recognized his calling: to help the weak to become as strong as he. And so he has gone on to his career, reproving inaccuracies, eradicating blunders, and chiding solecisms, as society expects of him. Even now, when linguistic values are no longer expressed solely in terms of righteousness, when the struggle to maintain Anglo-Saxon purity against the corruptions of Mediterranean and Slavic locutions has softened and become less urgent, and when correctness in social forms has all but vanished with the gentry, there still lingers the English teacher's obligation to uplift and reform the unenlightened. "Ooh! Are you an English teacher? I better watch what I say." Even those experienced teachers who try new approaches that are substitutes for correction return to the old way because otherwise they feel guilty that they are not really doing the job. It is therefore not surprising that, whenever it appears that writing is in a state of crisis and that students cannot write, there is an immediate public outcry for more correction. In such circumstances, few blame correction.

CORRECTION AND THE TEACHING LOAD

While believing unquestioningly in correction, teachers of English rarely find enough time for it. By the 1950s this frustration began to seek expression in speeches and articles about excessive enrollment and correction loads of members of the profession. In a tabulation of the responses by 430 experienced teachers in 150 California school districts to a questionnaire about loads and time spent in correcting papers, William J. Dusel figured that it took between 8.8 and 21.5 hours a week to mark papers of 250 words in length written by 150 students.[1] He also noted that English teachers have only a fraction of such time available during the school day, which they must devote to teaching, planning lessons, attending meetings, and handling clerical chores. Correction is therefore so large a burden after hours that it forces teachers either to decrease the number of writing assignments to too few or it causes them to correct papers hastily and superficially. In order to permit frequent writing and careful marking, Dusel proposed that English teachers be assigned four classes of no more than twenty-five students each and that the teachers be provided two daily periods to read and correct papers. Other surveys that followed made similar recommendations.

American education paid scant attention to calls for reduced English loads until the late 1950s and early 1960s, after Sputnik was lofted and the "war babies" began to crowd into high schools and colleges. Suddenly, there was a national will to surpass Russian technology by means of improved science teaching later extended to demands to upgrade the humanities by making them more rigorous and more like the European disciplines admired by Admiral H. G. Rickover. Articles appeared in newspapers and mass-circulated periodicals criticizing the life-adjustment curriculum and calling for the pursuit of excellence. Meanwhile, college instructors who were trying to cope with the enlarged student body protested that the high schools were failing to prepare young people adequately for college, particularly in writing. Others took up the cry. Corporation executives announced that their engineering personnel wrote so badly that it was necessary to hire professional writers to edit their reports. Professors of law and medicine expressed alarm at the inability of their graduate students to communicate. Editors, librarians, publishers, legislators, judges, and educators voiced dismay about the quality of English in their professions. "The teaching of English is so poor it has reached a desperate point that threatens the nation's educational system," warned a U.S. Commissioner of Education.[2] At the height of the uproar, the American Association of School Administrators, the Commission on English of the College Entrance Examination Board, the National Commission on Teacher Education, the NCTE, and the President's Commission on National Goals joined Harvard's former president Dr. James B. Conant in urging the allocation of more time to English teachers for more correcting of more compositions.

[1]William J. Dusel, "Determining an Efficient Teaching Load in English," *Illinois English Bulletin*, 43 (October 1955), pp. 1–19.
[2]Francis Keppel, quoted in *The New York Times*, December 30, 1963, p. 23.

IMPROVING CORRECTION

Even though political, technical, and pedagogical upheavals caused much dissatisfaction with the quality of writing, few persons questioned the immemorial way of teaching composition by means of correction. However, the impetus for excellence led to a realization that correction can be handled poorly. In addition, the new public interest in schooling opened what was happening in classrooms to citizens' scrutiny, including the teaching of writing. Consequently, the traditional purpose of correction, eliminating error, was augmented by a new goal: helping students to become better writers.

It was pointed out that poor correction has bad effects on students. When teachers disapprovingly label passages as clumsy or awkward or give poor and failing grades to themes, they discourage youngsters from wanting to write better, it was suggested. The use of proofreaders' symbols in correcting was also taken to task on the grounds that they show error but not how to overcome it. To add insult to injury, someone even asserted that the teacher who writes his corrections in broad pen strokes and oversized lettering is not merely drawing attention to his comments but also is expressing an irritability that is bound to arouse resentment in the novice writer. So the watchword for the 1960s was more time for better correction.

Besides advising against wrong correction practices, adherents of the new approach emphasized the positive. They felt that students would learn from correction, when they became receptive. To be accepted, correction would have to recognize and praise achievements. It would give high marks. It would stress ideas instead of errors, providing comments and questions as a guide to better writing. Unfortunately, teachers of English seem not to have implemented these strictures any more than their students have responded to corrections. In an investigation of composition teaching practices in 158 superior high schools during 1962 through 1968 James R. Squire and Roger K. Applebee found that two-thirds of thousands of compositions studied by observers had been annotated by teachers only for errors. The researchers commented that boys and girls cannot learn to write without proper correction.[3]

LAY-READERS

When professionals and laymen proposed reduced English loads for better correction, they, in effect, asked school districts to spend more money on English teaching. For every four teachers whose load was cut from five to four classes each, districts had to hire another teacher to absorb the aggregate of four classes taken from his colleagues. At, let us say, $7,000 a teacher per annum an English department of eight would cost $14,000 to provide a four-period load, and with perhaps 24 English teachers, a district would have to

---

[3] James R. Squire and Roger K. Applebee, *High School English Instruction Today: The National Study of High School English Programs* (New York: Appleton-Century-Crofts, 1968), p. 126.

come up with $42,000. Because few school districts could underwrite such expenditures, educators devised a less expensive and more immediate measure until such time as a community could afford to reduce loads. This was the lay-reader program. It assumed that college-educated housewives with writing ability could help to alleviate the English teacher's correction chores at low cost.

One of the earliest tests of the lay-reader method was begun in 1957 at the Newton High School, Massachusetts. Well received there, the plan was next taken up by the Concord and the Quincy schools. As the idea gained momentum, other districts engaged lay-readers. Soon its most enthusiastic advocates were describing it no longer as a temporary expedient but rather as an important innovation in teaching writing. They extolled the merits of the dedicated women who corrected papers, conferred with students, visited classrooms, rechecked revised papers, kept files of errors committed by individual pupils, and provided teachers with tabulations of frequent errors for use in classroom instruction.

Although the lay-readers plan attained a certain vogue, it did not become a national trend, as attested by its lack of consistent mention at annual meetings of the NCTE or in the Council's annual reports of promising practices. English teachers apparently did not see in it as fundamental an answer to their problems as reducing their teaching loads. In addition, the lay-reader programs themselves encountered difficulties. Some students complained that their English teachers were malingering. There were supervisors who murmured that some teachers neglected to use the readers' help to advantage. Other districts could not find interested and qualified housewives. Many readers found that it was difficult to work with writings of youngsters whom they did not meet or know. Although there were readers who accomplished much and even went on to become full-time teachers, the lay-reader idea did little to alter traditional correction practices.

What may be the program's basic deficiency is that, as the old way, it assumes that some kind of correction by adults of students' writings is what helps young people to write. Yet correcting does not seem to be effective in enough cases to merit the time and energy it consumes. Support for this conclusion can be found in the experiences of teachers and in the inferences of research.

WEAKNESSES IN CORRECTION

In the 1930s, studies of error counts in compositions revealed comma blunders and run-on sentences in all grade levels.[4] Today, after over thirty more years of correcting, certain errors like the run-on sentence can be noticed in almost every composition written by many students from grades seven through 13. The teacher who compares the papers of his students with those written at other grade levels is unable to discern any patent or gross differ-

[4]Henry C. Meckel, "Research on Teaching Composition and Literature," *Handbook of Research on Teaching*, N. L. Gage, editor (Chicago: Rand McNally & Company, 1963), p. 978.

ences in numbers of errors between lower and upper grades. Why does there appear to have been no growth or change? An answer is suggested by the national study mentioned,[5] which reported that a third of the compositions examined had not been revised in any manner whatsoever and that most students responded completely to corrections in only 12 percent of the schools that were sampled. It would appear that observation and normative studies do not find that correction does what correctors intend. And in an era of student unrest, few should be surprised that young people continue to ignore the written admonitions of their teachers of English regarding improved composition.

The small number of controlled experiments existing in the field of traditional correction also fail to support the method. A reading of their findings notes only one in favor, that of Earl W. Buxton, who, after an experiment during 1956 and 1957, concluded from an analysis of test scores of University of Alberta freshmen that thorough correction by teachers and then revision by students were superior to little correction and no revision.[6] Two other investigations, however, inferred the contrary. In 1931, John E. Fellows found no differences in counts of errors between papers corrected by teachers and papers given only letter marks, in a sampling of the writings of ninth graders in Iowa.[7] In 1961–1962, Lois V. Arnold and Dwight L. Burton were unable to determine any variations in the compositions of Florida tenth graders that could be related to low or high intensity of correction by teachers.[8]

Correction is undoubtedly time-consuming and apparently ineffectual. Yet the force of tradition and habit probably will continue to buttress it as the dominant trend in the teaching of writing. Asking an experienced teacher of English to refrain from editing spelling and other errors in his students' themes may be no more effectual than cautioning a husband to watch his language while giving his wife a driving lesson. Even if teachers were to deemphasize correction, there would be much explaining to parents who noticed uncorrected errors in their children's returned papers. The ideal solution to the problem would therefore be a method of teaching and learning writing that minimized the number of errors in the final product submitted for evaluation. Although no such panacea has been discovered as yet, some interesting alternatives may be at hand.

ALTERNATIVES TO CORRECTION

One promising departure is to train students to correct each other's or their own writing. Peer correction, which utilizes a novice writer's own classmates to scrutinize his work, assumes that adolescents can learn to write by

---

[5]Squire and Applebee, *High School English Instruction Today*, p. 122.

[6]Earl W. Buxton, "An Experiment to Test the Effects of Writing Frequency and Guided Practice upon Students' Skill in Written Expression," unpublished Ph.D. dissertation (Stanford, Calif.: Stanford University, 1958).

[7]John E. Fellows, *The Influence of Theme-Reading and Theme-Correction on Eliminating Technical Errors in the Written Compositions of Ninth-Grade Pupils*, Studies in Education, Vol. VII (Iowa City: University of Iowa, 1932).

[8]Lois V. Arnold and Dwight L. Burton, "Effects of Frequency of Writing and Intensity of Teacher Evaluation upon High School Students' Performance in Written Composition," unpublished Cooperative Research Project 1523, Florida State University, Tallahassee, 1963.

being motivated to write. It theorizes that adolescents are more receptive to the opinions of their contemporaries than to those of adult teachers; performing for an audience provides more of an incentive for writing than does performing for the teacher only. Although they do not occur often in professional literature, references to peer correction date as early as 1926, when Dora V. Smith used the method with a group of 51 ninth graders and concluded that it accomplished as much for them as did the traditional method for a class of 21.[9] Later, in the early 1950s, Ray C. Maize reported that a class of Purdue freshmen achieved more after frequent writing and peer correction than another class which wrote infrequent papers corrected by the instructor.[10] During 1964–1965 the author conducted an experiment with ninth graders in Syosset, New York, where he learned that students who submitted their compositions to peers for correction gained as much in writing-test scores as did others whose teachers evaluated their themes. He also found that peer correction used only an eighth of the time after hours that teachers devoted to correction.

Teachers who wish to try out peer correction have a number of variations from which to choose. In the Syosset program, the professional staff began by training students in the art of editing. To this end, they obtained samples of writings by pupils and also samples of corrections of these writings by classmates. Then they duplicated these materials, distributed them to classes, and conducted classroom discussions of the sample corrections, asking the groups to comment about the validity of the corrections and about their usefulness to the authors of the passages criticized. Next, the classes practiced correcting other sample papers. Afterwards, the teachers studied the corrections and told the novice critics of their achievements in editing and of their needs for improvement. When their students appeared familiar with the procedure, the teachers issued normal writing assignments to be corrected by classmates.

To assist the readers in their work, the teachers devised materials called guide sheets, which were often composed by the students themselves under the guidance of the adults. These sheets contained lists of ideas that served to tell each reader what to seek and what to say about his classmate's writing. A copy of a typical guide sheet is shown below. "Lines" refers to numbered lines for quick reference.

A Sample Guide Sheet for Comments about an Original Myth

Directions: Comment briefly and list numbers of lines that you are talking about.

Content

1. Does myth show a basic understanding and use of mythological characters and situations?

---

[9]Dora V. Smith, *Class Size in High School English* (Minneapolis: University of Minnesota Press, 1931).

[10]Ray C. Maize, "Two Methods of Teaching English Composition to Retarded College Freshmen," *Journal of Educational Psychology*, 45 (January, 1954), pp. 22–28.

2. Comment on the imagination and originality of the myth.
3. Is the myth logical? Is each new action tied in neatly with previous build-up in order to reach a logical outcome? Look for transitions from one idea to the next.
4. Does author give only a bare plot outline or does he develop story with imaginative details? Be specific in your comment pointing out where writer excelled or could improve his story.

Mechanics

1. If the person uses dialog, is it punctuated correctly? Or should dialog have been used instead of narrative?
2. In the following, make reference to specific lines in the myth that contain errors in spelling, sentence structure, punctuation, word choice, etc. Mention other weaknesses or strengths you may note.

Written by ———
Corrected by ———
Date ———

Boys and girls generally corrected one another's papers in groups of four or five, writing their critiques on guide sheets. On some occasions, members of the groups read their compositions to their fellows and heard verbal responses. At other times, several readers passed each theme around and wrote comments. When controversies arose between authors and their critics, the teachers arbitrated or suggested use of reference volumes, such as dictionaries and writing handbooks available in the classrooms. The teachers also encouraged peer groups to read to the whole class those papers that they regarded highly and to explain the reasons for their approval. In order to promote candid evaluation, critics were not asked to rate what they read. Teachers also tried to keep a balance between the numbers of able and weak students in each group and sometimes reshuffled members who did not mix well.

After the first three months of the experiment, which included classes that were taught writing traditionally, an observer read samples of compositions and corrections. In the groups practicing peer correction, he noted that many young readers had become skillful in finding mechanical, sentence, and paragraphing weaknesses. The mechanical difficulties that peers noticed included errors in punctuation, spelling, abbreviations, and manuscript conventions. In sentence matters, they found run-ons, fragments, and lack of sentence variety, one reader noting: "Your sentences should be different types instead of every one being the same." Among deficiencies in paragraphing found by peers was the absence of separate paragraphs for different speakers in written dialog.

On the negative side, the observer remarked that students had not learned well to correct mistakes in usage, diction, and organization. He pointed to infrequent correction of faulty pronoun reference. For example, three critics evaluated a paper containing this sentence: "He told everyone to go into their basement." In its context, the sentence should have had *his* instead of *their*. One reader did comment, "Words confused," but neither of the other two noticed any lack of agreement between pronoun and antecedent. However, when one considers the widespread use of *their* for *his*, he may not wish to judge the three readers harshly. In the category of errors in diction or word choice, few critics objected to needlessly repeated words. And when it came to helping classmates to organize content better, not many were equal to the task but confined themselves to such vague comments as "good, well-organized," even in cases when the truth was otherwise. Of course, critical abilities fell into a range of poor through good. For a typical example, in the case of two widely different readings of the same composition, one listed abundant references to mechanical and sentence errors, while the other recorded no mistakes at all.

Near the end of the school year, the observer read samples again and concluded that students in peer groups had made progress in learning how to correct errors in diction but less so in usage and in organization. He also sensed a tendency on the part of young writers to accept mistaken peer corrections, a testimonial to the strength of the peer influence. The most dramatic effect of the correcting experience on the readers was evidently a heightened awareness of writing which lacks audience appeal.

One of the composition assignments that was written during the experiment was the following editorial:

> Most of half a year of school have past. Day after day I have gone to the same room.
> All my subject classes are interesting and amusing, but then I have lunch. In the lunch room I eat with my fellow companions. By now, although I still like them I am getting tired of them and the surrounding area.
> I fell, if we had a bright new murals they would lift our morales and attitudes. And would certianly make the lunch room and lunches for the 40 min. we are there more enjoyable and interesting.

A classmate of the writer responded to the composition as follows: "Sloppy. Margins O.K. Paragraphs indented O.K. Don't abbrev. min. Fell should be feel. Mural not murals. No basic facts all appeal to emotions. It would be nice to have a new mural but it's not that important to put in the school newspaper. There is so much going on in the lunchroom I never had time to notice the murals."

The foregoing is an example of how a student writer can obtain a response from a peer with respect to mechanics, paragraphing, and ideas. Who can say that such an experience, even though incomplete, does less for writing than does receiving his teacher's criticisms, which can point out more errors and can make suggestions for improvements in the rhetoric of persuasion and in organization?

Teachers who participated in the experiment suffered corrector's guilt when they saw the omissions of peer critics. Their own commissions, however, were sometimes clearly wasted. In one essay, a boy concluded a description of sense impressions of a beach with the words, "I knew this was the end!" His teacher wrote in the margin, "Of the world? of summer? the ultimate experience?" In his revision, the student changed the sentence as follows: "I knew this was the end of the ultimate experience." Maybe a clearer comment would have avoided this amusing contretemps. Yet the boy might still have revised incorrectly through lack of concern. Maybe he would have paid more attention to a correction by a classmate. Perhaps there should have been more follow-up by the teacher.

Since the conclusion of their experiment, the teachers have occasionally combined the traditional method with peer correction. When busy with the tasks of starting a semester, they prefer the old way, because it requires no new training efforts. When the pressure of work lets up, they then introduce the peer method. In a more immediate form of combination, they divide the labor of correction with their students, who correct each other's mechanical, sentence, and paragraph errors, while their instructors assess more difficult matters, such as usage, diction, and organization.

After trying peer correction in Texas, Sherry Zively noticed that it helped students to perceive flaws in composition better than reading texts on writing, outlining themes on the chalkboard, receiving extensive correction from the teacher, and revising mistakes. The instructor also used an element of psychology with C and D writers, who thought themselves to be good; they learned to be realistic about their own efforts by correcting superior papers. To prevent the confused from correcting the confused, good writers graded poor ones.[11]

An instructor of college freshmen, Michael Grady, became dissatisfied with his corrections because he found that a repeated error in a paper unduly influenced and distorted his evaluation. As an alternative, he devised a system whereby writers became their own critics. At the beginning of the semester, he corrected themes in order to acquaint the class with his writing standards. Later on he gave the group a set of guide questions about mechanics, diction, organization, and logic; students used these to assess their own efforts. Errors decreased, he inferred, because self-esteem prevented recurrence. Self-correction also made the students curious to attend conferences with the instructor to find out how their own corrections compared with his. He noted, however, that they failed to notice errors of logic and agreement. They furthermore gave themselves needlessly low marks.[12] Perhaps corrections without grades would have avoided this problem.

Some critics point out that correction as conventionally practiced fails because students ignore it. Others say that what is most at fault is that correction emphasizes the product and not the process of writing. Robert Zoellner has attracted attention recently by concentrating on the act of writing and by using talking skills to build writing skills. If he had his way, writing classrooms would resemble art studios and have many blackboards or large pads

[11]Sherry Zively, "A Cautious Approach to Student Grading," *English Journal*, 56 (December, 1967), pp. 1321–1322.

[12]Michael Grady, "A Technique for Theme Correction," *Classroom Practices in Teaching English: A Fifth Report of the NCTE Committee on Promising Practices* (Champaign, Ill.: NCTE, 1967), pp. 77–81.

of newsprint on easels, on which learners would write with chalk or felt pens under the surveillance of peers and the teacher. The latter would ask questions and make remarks while the writers would respond in a continuing dialog. Writers would also observe fluent classmates and the instructor in demonstrations of writing, particularly as they phrased, hesitated, rephrased, verbalized, crossed out, failed, and started again, encouraging similar efforts by their examples. Zoellner believes that desired responses may be reinforced immediately and indeed conditioned by immediate recognition of achievement in contrast to the delayed return of corrections under the old system.[13]

Zoellner's imaginative approach to teaching writing merits the attention of the English profession not only because of the advantages he attributes to it but also because it may release powers of motivation already noted in peer-correction and lacking in the conventional method. His approach may also have its attractions for teachers who despair of alternatives to correction, which are few. However, they must also heed warnings that talk-writing may be founded in some degree on questionable premises. It assumes that students are better talkers than writers and that there can be a successful transfer of training from the one form of expression to the other. Considering that many of the conventions of writing, such as spelling, indenting paragraphs, capitalizing, and punctuating, are foreign to speech, one hesitates to make writing from talking. The tendencies of normal speech to run sentences together, to fragment, to change directions in mid-sentence, intensified by the vagueness, incoherence, and triteness of youthful oralism (not to mention the apocalyptic rhetoric of the New Left) do not hold much promise for useful transfer of training.

The following excerpt from a letter by Thomas Jefferson about George Washington suggests that it could be mistaken to believe that talking comes easier than writing to all:

> Although in the circle of his friends, where he might be unreserved with safety, he took a free share in conversation, his colloquial talents were not above mediocrity, possessing neither copiousness of ideas, nor fluency of words. In public, when called on for a sudden opinion, he was unready, short, and embarrassed. Yet he wrote readily, rather diffusely, in an easy and correct style. This he had acquired by conversation with the world, for his education was merely reading, writing, and common arithmetic, to which he added surveying at a later day. His time was employed in action chiefly, reading little, and that only in agriculture and English history. His correspondence became necessarily extensive, and, with journalizing his agricultural proceedings, occupied most of his leisure hours within doors.[14]

In fact, Zoellner's classroom studio would do well to encourage participants to write notes to one another, if Washington's example is still valid.

---

[13]Robert Zoellner, "Talk-Write: A Behavioral Pedagogy for Composition," *College English*, 30 (January 1969), pp. 267–320.

[14]Thomas Jefferson, letter to Dr. Walter Jones, January 2, 1814, quoted by Sculley Bradley, Richmond C. Beatty, and E. Hudson Long, editors, *The American Tradition in Literature*, third edition, vol. I (New York: Grosset and Dunlap, Inc., 1967), pp. 335–36.

There also is some reason to believe that the effect of psychological conditioning of responses varies with the personality of the conditioner, which in education would mean that the method is only as good as the teacher. Another limitation of conditioning is that, when reinforcement stops, responses become weaker and eventually disappear. Nonetheless, despite limitations, attention to the writing process may yield unexpected treasures for the teacher of writing.

SUMMARY

The teaching of writing has depended largely and, to the author's way of thinking, excessively on a single method of instruction because of custom and public expectations. This method, correcting papers, has been reinforced and proliferated during recent years by national concern for the quality of writing. Such concern has generated programs for more and better correction and for reduced correcting loads for teachers of English, either through fewer pupils assigned or through help from lay-readers. Although peer-correction, self-correction, and talk-writing offer promising alternatives, it is expected that the immediate future will find teachers continuing to correct papers dutifully (or cursorily) despite research findings to the contrary and evidence of indifference on the part of students. Continued efforts therefore will be needed to make the system work. One way to do so is to employ the composition conference, which prevents correction from being wasted.

THE COMPOSITION CONFERENCE

IV

In many schools the teacher of English assigns a composition, receives and corrects it, returns it to the writer, and then forgets about it. The five-to-fifteen minutes that he has invested in reading and correction turn to account, hopefully, when the student writes his next theme. If this hope is vain, the investment is lost, and the act of correction is wasted motion. Occasionally, the teacher uses a corrected theme for a purpose other than discarding or filing. He may put an outstanding piece of writing into a scrapbook or on a bulletin board. He may even suggest that the author submit it to the school newspaper, literary magazine, or yearbook. But all too rarely does it happen that the teacher uses students' written work as the starting point of a lesson in composition or as the topic of a personal conference with the writer.

When James B. Conant published his report to interested citizens called *The American High School Today*, he proposed that schools give English teachers no more than 100 students, to allot the teachers enough time to correct an average of one composition per student weekly.[1] During the years that followed, a number of school districts undertook such a program and earmarked released time to conduct writing conferences. This emphasis illustrates the high regard in which conferences are held by laity and professionals alike. Current professional literature in the teaching of writing gives consistently warm approval to this procedure.

> The use of conferences during the school day as an evaluation procedure is increasing in popularity.[2]
>
> . . . such an activity is an important adjunct to the successful teaching of composition.[3]
>
> Perhaps the most successful practice in the teaching of composition has been the regular conference to discuss the problems and progress of the individual student.[4]

[1] James B. Conant, *The American High School Today* (New York: McGraw-Hill, 1959), p. 51.
[2] William H. Evans and Jerry L. Walker, *New Trends in the Teaching of English in Secondary Schools* (Chicago: Rand McNally, 1966), p. 57.
[3] Richard Corbin, *The Teaching of Writing in Our Schools* (New York: Macmillan, 1966), p. 90.
[4] James R. Squire and Roger K. Applebee, *High School English Instruction Today: The National Study of High School English Programs* (New York: Appleton-Century-Crofts, Educational Division, Meredith Corporation, 1968), p. 254.

Yet, despite high regard, no carefully formulated theory and methodology of conferring has thus far appeared in the pedagogy of English. In other professions, such as personnel service, guidance, and psychology practitioners have developed much knowledge about the conference. A beginning in English might be made by means of systematic investigation, using recordings of composition conferences.

A TRANSCRIPT OF A CONFERENCE

A teacher of English in junior high school recently made an audiotape of a ten-minute session that she held with a ninth year student. What follows is a verbatim transcript of their conversation concerning three of the girl's compositions.

Teacher: I have three essays I want to talk to you about. I want to say first of all that you read very well, and you know what you're reading about, and you make some very good points. You certainly understand what the conflict was in this story about Fiona. And in this article on a group of short stories you read, I thought this was a very good point: the fact that you became involved with the Thurber story, because you could identify with the family. He let you in on their secrets, and therefore you could identify with the family, and then that made it so much more real and enjoyable, so you really know what you're reading, and you have things to say about it. Now you have to work on organizing what you're going to say. And then you have to work on saying it clearly and not wordily. You're using too many words that get in your way and that make for awkward sentences and that clutter up your writing. Let's talk, first of all, about organizing, because that's a difficult task. I really organized this paragraph for you all, because I told you I want you to pick out the conflict and write about the conflict. And you did. You gave me a good controlling . . . a sentence with a controlling idea. "The conflict was within Fiona: should she be her own person or remain a carbon copy?" That's good. That is your controlling idea. Now, what must your paragraph be about, if that is what you're going to talk about?

Pupil: Well, I have to prove it. My point.

Teacher: Right. You have to prove it. How . . . how are you going to prove it in this story?

Pupil: By giving examples of how she was made a carbon copy. And her attempts to try and be her own person.

Teacher: Right. That is, that's all you're going to do in this paragraph. But you didn't. You went off the track. You started talking about her grandfather. Um . . . "In the end when Fiona is outside and called inside, she doesn't answer." Well, you've told us after the conflict's been resolved how she acts.

Pupil: Well, this is how I showed that she's now become her own person; when she doesn't answer, that means she has a mind of her own, because, before that, she'd always answered right away, one-two-three, you know, when her parents called, and now she feels I don't have to answer right away.

Teacher: Very true. But that would be another paragraph in which you would then show how she resolves the conflict. But that wasn't the subject of this paragraph. The subject was what is the conflict? not how was it resolved? So stick to that idea only in your paragraph. Don't go on to something else. The same with this one on the short stories. Um . . . first of all, you had trouble deciding what your controlling idea was and saying it clearly. I think you were trying to say that the way a good short story writer makes you care about his story is by making it so real and so natural that it's believable and you can become involved in it. Isn't that what you were saying, something like that?

Pupil: That's right.

Teacher: And you did back it up when you talked about the Thurber story. But then it seemed to me that you lost track of that idea, and you went off into other ideas when it came to the other stories.

Pupil: Where?

Teacher: "Frank Stockton's 'A Piece of Red Calico' does not fulfill the effect he tries to set." Well, what has that got to do with the fact that a story must be real enough for you to be involved with?

Pupil: You see, I was trying to prove that a good short story to me is one that makes me feel right. You know, that you're right in there. And he was giving too many details. Like he was getting the reader confused by so many details explaining everything that happened. And I think he was trying to make it sound real, but I don't think he accomplished it. That's what I meant by that.

Teacher: All right. Good. Good, because that's really backing up your point. But that's what you've got to tell us. And you haven't told us that. That would be fine. We have to know what's going on in your mind. The way you wrote it, it sounded as though you were jumping onto another subject altogether. Now let's talk about . . . oh, well, now here's a case where you're being irrelevant. "In reverse, a writer of short stories who is knowledgeable about life can eventually write . . . fiction?"

Pupil: Fictionous.

Teacher: Fictionous? There's no such word.

Pupil: (Embarrassed laughter.) Fictitious?

Teacher: Fictitious, maybe that's the word . . . "fictitious and non-fiction stories with related ideas about life."

Pupil: I think I'm trying . . . I don't remember this remark. I think I'm trying to say that if he starts out with this he can make, um, other stories that are true. Like these are. He made them up. Some of them. And he could now take, uh, things that really happened and, you know, like sometimes like the Civil War or something, sometimes they're, uh, drab and like you don't feel . . . like I'm just reading history. You could feel that, uh, you're in there, you're fighting the war; this is what I meant by that. He could make this realism happen in, um, things that did happen in history.

Teacher: All right. Very good point, but you have to say it so that I know that that's what you're saying. And in the third one, the one on revenge, I never could find, um, your thesis. I feel from reading your examples that your thesis was revenge is sweet. The people in the three stories that I'm writing about enjoy their revenge. It was satisfying to them. Isn't that, wasn't that your thesis?

Pupil: Yes.

Teacher: But you start out first of all in a way which is going to turn me off as a reader, because you're sort of being very patronizing. You're saying let us delve further into the satisfying emotion with hopes that all may fully understand it. You know: come, dear children, now let us . . . uh, isn't that the sound that it has? It's um, um, that's not your task to . . . I mean it isn't as though you're a great knowledgeable person, and you're going to take all of us ignoramuses and, and lead us down the path of knowledge. Your, your job is to talk very seriously and straightforwardly about three stories in which you felt that revenge was proved to be very sweet.

Pupil: I think I was trying to make it sound like a fairy tale like, um, do you ever listen how they all start out? Um, soandso happened in the beautiful warm climate . . . I think that's what I was trying to do.

Teacher: All right. In a critical essay like this I don't think, I don't think it goes, not the way you've done it, anyway. Maybe, maybe it could be used, especially if you were using it in the same style as, as something you were writing about, but I don't know about here. Um, so that I never did fully, fully get this statement of this thesis. And you end up in the same patronizing way. "As we look at the facts clearly, we can see that etc." You know people resent being talked to like that, don't you think?

Pupil: I think so.

Teacher: Right. O.K. Ah, I think in the future you've got to think before you start writing. Say to yourself what am I going to talk about? And put it in a sentence, in a good sentence. This is what I'm going to talk about and this only. And everything else I say in this essay is going to back up this main idea. And be sure you state your idea very clearly. If you want to then start making it a little more snappy or, or interesting, you can rewrite it. But be sure it says clearly what you're gonna talk about. Ah, let's talk also about some of this wordiness which I think is one of your problems. "Writers of short stories have many ways to make their stories remain in our minds as one of the best." Why do you need "as one of the best"?

Pupil:	The thing I was trying to say, like, by this, writers in many ways can make their stories stay in our minds. Like it was not a good st . . . like it's possible that we can remember a story because it was bad. I'm trying to say that these stories stay in our mind because we enjoyed them so much.
Teacher:	Well, why not just say, "Writers of short stories have many ways to make their story remain in our mind"? You don't need "as one of the best." It throws us off and is not necessary. "Characterization, mystery, and details all help, but a realistic feeling . . ." There's where you've got to start using a dictionary or a thesaurus to find out how you would express "a realistic feeling," because that is not a succinct way to put it.
Pupil:	Is it too general?
Teacher:	"A realistic feeling." It's too general, too nebulous. Uh, but realism, if you just said realism, naturalism, um, but, as I said here, what I think you really are trying to say is "but when we can identify with a character in a situation, then he's done a job." I think that's what you were trying to say. Um, "minute trivia." Why "minute trivia"? Why not just "trivia."?
Pupil:	(Laughter.)
Teacher:	You know you're overdoing it. "He tries to involve the reader in the confusing actions of a man who is trying to match up two pieces of red calico." Just repeating the word trying, try and trying, get a better word for trying here.
Pupil:	Oh, yes.
Teacher:	It's just that it hits my ear, and I hear try. That's all I hear; it's the double try. Sometimes repeating a word is very important. But there it's just cluttering up your writing. Um, this is awkward. (Bell sounds.) Oh, I know you've got to go, don't you?
Pupil:	I have study hall.
Teacher:	All right. I'll be a little late for the class. "His purpose wanders and he misguides the reader, instead. By this one has no feeling of time or place."
Pupil:	That's what I meant by he was throwing in too many details.
Teacher:	Yes.
Pupil:	Uh, this man was like running . . . to a zillion stores in like one minute and we were getting all confused and you didn't know what time it was . . .
Teacher:	All right. I'm not objecting to what you're saying. I'm just objecting to how you're saying it. "His purpose wanders." "His purpose wanders." "He wanders" rather than "the purpose wanders." "He wanders and misguides the reader."
Pupil:	I think, I think . . .
Teacher:	"So that," why not, why not, why end the sentence and then say, "by this"? That's so awkward.

Pupil: That would be a run-on.

Teacher: No, that isn't a run-on. "So that" is a conjunction that joins a dependent
              clause. "He wanders and misguides the reader so that one has no feeling
              of time or place." Isn't that clearer and flows better?

Pupil: Yes.

Teacher: O.K. Thanks. I'll get back to you a bit later.

Pupil: O.K.

The reader of the foregoing transcript can readily infer that it concerns
three compositions the girl has written about short stories that she has read.
The teacher's remarks emphasize ways in which the writer can attain unity
and relevance in her paragraphs and clarity, economy, and appropriate tone
in her diction. Although the teacher carries most of the burden of the conversation, the girl responds, asks questions, and explains her writing.

THE TEACHER'S REMARKS

What is the value of this interview? An answer may come from a look at
the writing that led to the conference and at the corrections and comments
inserted by the teacher. The compositions will be referred to as Fiona, Thurber-Stockton, and Revenge and are shown in sequence in Figures 1, 2, and 3.

"Stick to the subject. What is the conflict?" and "not part of this paragraph" are comments written in the margins of Fiona (Fig. 1). The author
asked the young writer if she remembered what her response was to these
entries when she first read them. She replied that, at the time, she did not
understand the second annotation, "not part of this paragraph." However, after
her teacher told her that her paragraph about the story's conflict should not
have included a reference to the resolution of the conflict, the annotation became clear. Of course, one may argue that it is entirely arbitrary whether or
not to refer to the resolution, when developing a paragraph about the conflict in a work of fiction. It is nonetheless true that the teacher's remarks in
conference explained the composition assignment for the student as the
teacher had conceived it, where the written comments failed. The teaching of
composition is sometimes too abstract to help students satisfactorily to perform the specific and even unique tasks that are the consequence of an assignment applied to an entire class. Although all members of a class in physics
must perform the same operations to measure the behavior of matter in a
laboratory exercise, no two English students ever write the same composition.
Many boys and girls are therefore baffled by their inability to meet their
teachers' requirements while struggling to compose an original statement,
despite the best of will. Although writing, as an act of personal creation, must
remain a lonely chore, the conference can help the student better to understand what is expected of him. And by revealing to the teacher the students'
writing problems that she has failed to anticipate, the conference enables her
to assign more feasible writing next time.

In the second paragraph of Thurber-Stockton (Fig. 2), the teacher writes

Stick to the subject – what is the conflict?

Fiona was a child physically, but mentally she was being forced to relive her mother's and grandmother's childhood. The conflict was within Fiona; should she be her own person or remain ~~becoming~~ a carbon copy? She was forced to eat, dress and talk the way her elders did, but not allowed to grow up like a normal child. Her mind was debating if she should explore the outside world. When she answered "yes" she was on ~~here~~ her way to being herself with her own mind. When walking down the road she stopped at the Fadgins house and spent the day there. On returning home she was upset for going against her parents, but was also glad she had made up her own mind. In the end when Fiona is outside and called inside she does not answer. This shows she has learned something very valuable from the Fadgins. This was to be herself by acting and talking that way.

Not part of this ¶

FIGURE 1
Fiona

You back up your thesis well with the Thurber example. In the others you sometimes lose sight of your controlling idea. Don't be wordy.

Writers of short stories have many ways to make their story remain in our minds (as one of the best.) Characterization, m?ystery and details all help but (a realistic feeling) assists the story the most. When one gets involved in the problem of the story (itself) one can (actually) jump in and take the place of a character.

realism? naturalism? I think the phrase you're looking for is "Identification with character and situation"

¶ James Thurber has acheived (sp) this in "The Night the Bed Fell." It's (sp) homely atmosphere leaps? out and engulfs you. (When compared with "A Piece of Red Calico" his outstanding details shine through moreso.) With a set of eccentric aunts, uncles, and cousins, Thurber describes their pecularities. For example, one aunt piled up shoes at her door each night just in case a burglar might try to rob her. Another kept a glass of spirits of camphor by his bed so that if he stopped breathing in his

doesn't belong here

K

What does this phrase modify?

FIGURE 2
Thurber-Stockton

sleep he would be revived ~~Minute~~ *rep.*
Trivia like this is usually the
guarded secret~~s~~? of each ~~Particular~~
family. When one shares these
secrets, he feels as if he is a
part of the family. *good point*

Frank Stockton's "A Piece of Red
Calico" does not forfeit the effect
he tries to ~~get~~? He tries *rep.* to involve
the reader in the confusing actions
of a man who is trying *rep.* to match
up two pieces of red calico. His
purpose wanders and he misguides
the reader instead, *so that* ~~Dig this~~, one
has no feeling of time or place.
The story leads us to an ironic
ending, but Thurber's finish was
more enjoyable by its character's
misunderstandings.

The next two stories are ~~quite~~
similar *to what?* in the way they're written.
When reading "Little Gentleman" it *rf.*
was like seeing a movie of someone's
little brother on a trip for a haircut.

what wanders?

FIGURE 2 (continued)

had continually been annoyed by Slade, Slade was ~~wartly~~ of his revenge. Baumer was shrewd ~~by~~ changing his order of alcohol to wood alcohol. Since Slade couldn't read, he drank this poison, ~~which goes to show that~~ Baumer was smart to strike at his Achilles's heel. Baumer's revenge too was sweet, for now with no fear of a bully, he could continue his life and business peacefully.

When we stop to think about the story "Haircut," we must also think of the type of revenge used. Jim, the prankster had nothing against half-witted Paul, but against Doc. Being a friend of Doc's, Paul felt just as bad. When Jim and Paul went on a fishing trip together, Paul killed him. This revenge is different than most for nothing was done to Paul, yet he suffered as much as the victim. Therefore this killing was the revenge of both Doc and Paul and was sweet for both, too.

[margin annotations: RWW "wartly" ; WW "in" ; "You don't need this" ; "Statements like this sound rather pompous + phony" ; "but this isn't what you're discussing" ; "Not clear." ; "Why? How?"]

FIGURE 2 (continued)

You don't need this

As we look at the facts clearly, [P] we can see that All the avengers *in the stories* *considered* are satisfied by killing or hurting their enemies. Therefore, it is evident that revenge is sweet, even sweeter than flowing honey.

FIGURE 2 (continued)

a question mark above *set* and underlines this word in the sentence, "Frank Stockton's 'A Piece of Red Calico' does not forfill the effect he tries to set." These annotations leave the writer to her own devices to find out what is incorrect and what to do about it. One does not set an effect but creates one. In conference, the teacher leapfrogs this rather mechanical matter and concentrates on the more complex issue of developing the whole theme around a controlling idea, which she has already begun to examine in her remarks about the Fiona paragraph (Fig. 1). She proceeds to explain that the sentence does not relate to the controlling idea that realism involves the reader. When the girl reveals that the story does not make her feel right, the teacher now understands that "A Piece of Red Calico" was not credible to the student and hence did not engage her emotions. For her part, the pupil now sees that her sentence did not convey this message to her reader.

In this exchange, the teacher has helped her student to comprehend a principle of writing that applies to several of her compositions. In addition, it has been possible to attend to more than mere correctness. The conference has also provided the young writer with an opportunity to justify her ideas and to bring about her teacher's understanding of them, an opportunity not usually afforded by means of written correction. In the student's own words, "I had a chance to explain what I meant." Her feelings may be appreciated by those adults who will recall their own unfulfilled yearnings to reply upon retrieval of college term papers annotated by professors.

" 'Let us' is patronizing and turns your readers away," writes the teacher in a margin of the Revenge paper (Fig. 3). This may suffice to alert the writer to her failure to anticipate the effect of her words on a reader. However, if not, then surely in conference, she learns it from the dramatic intonation of the teacher's mimicry in "you know; come, dear children." Awareness of the need to write in consideration of an emotionally responsive audience is a foreign idea to many students who have become habituated to approaching a writing assignment as they do a chore (walking the dog or putting the garbage out), something to be concluded as mechanically and as quickly as possible. In a recent conference with her teacher, a student responded to the idea of audience consideration with surprise and commented that, had she been writing for an audience, she would have proceeded far differently when composing her theme. Students must learn to write for their readers; the conference, while not the only means, can provide a sense of audience.

In summary, the composition interview permits teachers to explain aspects of writing that require more information than written correction can afford. It also is useful in clarifying and in improving the assignment process, as well as in encouraging writing for an audience. Of no less importance is the fact that the conference can serve as the student's outlet for expression and means of justification, moving communication in two directions rather than exclusively from teacher to pupil.

Mrs. L., who had volunteered to supply the author with the aforementioned audiotape was modestly disconcerted when she read the written transcript; to her, her ellipses and hesitations seemed awkward, possibly because, unaware, she was holding what was in effect a written and therefore imper-

("Let us" is patronising & turns your readers away)

You must stick to one idea & develop it carefully.

Your essay that follows only delves into the idea that revenge is sweet. That is your thesis & must be so stated in your opening ¶.

as defined by the

Revenge ~~as quoted from~~ Thorndike-Barnhart dictionary is "harm done for a wrong; vengence." [sp] Let us dealve [sp] further into this satisfying emotion, with hopes that all may fully understand it.

The short stories we have read (without a doubt) prove that revenge indeed is sweet. For an example, let us take the story "Bernice Bobs Her Hair." Bernice's revenge on her cousin Majorie was just. When Bernice said she would bob her hair she was only trying to start a conversation. Knowing this, Majorie challanged [sp] her by saying she [ref] was bluffing. If Bernice didn't cut her hair she might lose her reputation so she had to do it. Majorie was the indirect cause. Revenge is sweet, for Bernice his [x] the satisfaction of evening up the scores.

Another story which proves revenge is sweet is "Bargain." Since Baumer

FIGURE 3
Revenge

Booth Tarkington most likely knows little boys very well for the grunting and squealing noises by the boy in the barber's chair ~~just~~ added to it's realism. Telling us about Penrod's escapades around town and with a barrel of tar makes one stop and think if her son has ever done that.

"The Night the Ghost Got In" by James Thurber projects an unmistakable comical air, too. Although this story was enjoyable, such misunderstandings are not usual. ~~By this~~ ~~Hearing~~ noises does not lead one to call the police in fear a ghost might be lurking ~~about~~. "Little Gentleman" seems more down to earth possibly because almost anything children do or say in stories can happen in life.

Life and short stories can go hand in hand. If one reads short stories he can ~~possibly~~ perhaps understand his own life better

FIGURE 3 (continued)

46

through
~~by~~ the trials and errors of
others. Although the incidents
may not be the same, they
may prove to be relevant. In
reverse, a writer of short stories
who is knowledgeable about life
can eventually write (fiction ~~ous~~ *do you need this?* and
non-fiction ~~ous~~) stories with related
ideas about life. But one fact
remains; true life and her
details are the best mystery,
adventure and novel stories that
ever can be written.

what does this have to do with your thesis?

not clear

FIGURE 3 (continued)

fect translation of her spoken words up to the standards of deliberate and polished writing. She agreed, however, that recording helped her to improve her conference procedures. Because they do not usually hear themselves as others do, teachers may refine their interview methods by using the tape recorder occasionally. They may also benefit from a consideration of attributes and procedures demonstrated by Mrs. L.

First, Mrs. L. knows writing, having the advantage of work experience in publications. And even in so small a body as the foregoing conference, teachers may discern her familiarity with the following: literary criticism, organization of the elements of a composition, sources for improving diction, and fundamentals of grammar. Second, she uses a number of exemplary techniques in her conduct of the interview. She has prepared for it by gathering beforehand a group of the student's papers that illustrate interrelated problems and by earmarking specific passages to be used to demonstrate general principles. She aptly interviews rather than only lectures thereby encouraging the student to think and to respond. Third, Mrs. L.'s approach is systematic; she makes a record of the conference for future reference, using a form published in her department for this purpose. (Fig. 4.)

On this blank she has placed a check in the *strength* column opposite *quality and degree of development of ideas* and checks in the weakness column opposite *organization, sentence structure,* and *word choice.*[5] Her statement after *comments* is as follows:

---

[5]Categories of writing skill used on the form were adapted from a list formulated by Paul B. Diederich, Educational Testing Service, Princeton, New Jersey.

RECORD OF COMPOSITION CONFERENCE

Teacher _____ Date _____ Per _____

Student's Name _____

STRENGTH		WEAKNESS
	Quality and degree of development of ideas	_____
_____	**ORGANIZATION**	
_____	Introduction	_____
_____	Transitions	_____
_____	Paragraphing	_____
_____	Conclusion	_____
	MECHANICS	
_____	Usage	_____
_____	Capitalization	_____
_____	Punctuation	_____
_____	Spelling	_____
_____	Handwriting	_____
	STYLE	
_____	Sentence Structure	_____
_____	Word Choice	_____

Comments: _____

_____

_____

_____

_____

_____

_____

_____

_____

FIGURE 4

All three compositions we'll discuss are about short stories. You show a good understanding of what you read. You need to be sure to express your controlling idea clearly and then to limit your essay to a discussion of that idea. You haven't stuck to your controlling idea in the paper on outside reading—and you haven't expressed the idea clearly. Don't *over-write*, ex., "minute trivia," "actually," "each particular," "quite similar."

The student has access to this record in her composition folder. Fourth and last, Mrs. L. knows how to reach the young, as evidenced by the warmth of the exchange between her and the girl, who feels that the conversation is important enough to extend into her study-hall period.

A THEORY AND PRACTICE OF THE CONFERENCE

As more writing interviews are analyzed in professional literature, teachers of writing may develop an elaborated and systematized structure and guide to follow, when they meet with their students in writing conferences. To generate a proper theory and practice, they can benefit from the findings of counselors and psychologists, who use the interview as a basic procedure for helping clients. There is much discussion in these professions of whether the counseling approach should be directive or non-directive. Those who prefer to be directive tend to the didactic and prescriptive or even the critical and admonitory in relating to clients. It is their belief that, knowing more than any client by virtue of training and experience, they must diagnose his problem and give him the remedy. Nondirective or, as some prefer, client-centered workers believe that attitudes and behavior do not change in response to prescription, which causes the client instead to resist what he sees as intimidating and perturbing. "There seems to be sufficient evidence that threat results in impairment of learning and reasoning to warrant being cautious in the use of direct, active methods, which might constitute a threat."[6] Nondirection also assumes that people with difficulties can help themselves, when they are freed from emotional impediments.

Granted that a procedure for dealing with emotional problems cannot be applied naively to the solution of writing problems, which are highly intellectual, there is however a good possibility that children, especially today, respond more easily to their relationship with a teacher than to his powers of logic or persuasion. If so, teachers of composition should avoid remarks in conference that cause anxiety and should attempt other means of changing writing behavior. They can make efforts to convey to students an attitude of empathy and understanding. Teachers of composition can also try to encourage the student to take initiatives in evaluating and in finding ways of improving his own writing. How can this be done? Possibly by adopting and adapting such nondirective procedures as structuring, clarification of feeling, acceptance, approval, reassurance, and nondirective leads.

By structuring, counselors mean statements that aid the client in understanding what is happening, what may be anticipated of both participants

[6]C. H. Patterson, *Theories of Counseling and Psychotherapy* (New York: Harper & Row, 1966), p. 133.

during the conference, when the conference can be expected to end, and what outcome may ensue. These comments by Mrs. L. classify structuring: "I have three essays I want to talk to you about." "Let's talk first of all about organizing." "Oh, I know you've got to go, don't you?" Structuring appears to be valuable in almost any interview, directive or not, as an alternative to unplanned or even rambling comments by an English teacher, which confuse the student about purposes, procedures, and consequences.

In order to help the client to understand his own feelings and to assure him that his listener appreciates his reasons for them, the counselor rephrases the client's utterances in clearer language or simply identifies the client's feelings. Referring to the cited, taped interview, where Mrs. L.'s student said, "This man was like running . . . to a zillion stores in like one minute, etc.," Mrs. L. replied, "I'm not objecting to what you're saying. I'm just objecting to how you're saying it." Nondirectively she might first have responded: "Yes, it used to be considered good writing to include long descriptions and complicated actions, but today we like writers to come immediately to the point, don't we?" Or more simply, "I see that this kind of writing annoyed you." In addition to clarifying feelings, this technique in the writing conference may be useful in clarifying thought and in providing the novice writer with a larger stock of language choices for his or her repertory.

To give the client confidence in himself, counselors employ acceptance, approval, and reassurance. Acceptance is merely agreement that expresses comprehension but no value judgment. This can be a plain "yes" or "no" (after a negative) or a "That's true." Approval is, of course, agreement that implies concurrence, as shown in the following examples from Mrs. L.'s interview:

Pupil:	"Well, I have to prove it. My point."
Teacher:	"Right. You have to prove it."
Pupil:	"That's what I meant by that."
Teacher:	"All right. Good. Good, because that's really backing up your point."

Reassurance expresses sympathy with the client. "I understand why you feel that way." "I think I would react the same way as you did." "That wasn't fair at all." Or, in response to the student previously mentioned, who says, "I think that's what I was trying to do," the teacher can comment, "Oh, I think I see now what you were after. A take-off on stories that end happily for the hero." When a fledgling writer is trying to execute a *chandelle* for the teacher, it is necessary for his tutor to take notice, even if the maneuver is somewhat tacky.

Nondirective leads are a technique used to encourage the client to talk about his difficulties and also to assume the initiative in shaping the course of the conversation. "How do you see it?" "Can you say this another way?" "What is your thesis?" "In which of these compositions did you succeed best? Why?" "Which gave you the most trouble?" Although many secondary teachers are expert at asking questions, too often these are directed towards a preconceived answer. Open-ended questions can help young writers think for themselves.

The use of nondirective techniques in writing conferences may provide an antidote for traditional overdirection, teacher-centered talk, and under-motivation. They may help students to become receptive to teachers' ideas about composition; they may also serve to make students feel more adequate as writers. At the very least, a knowledge of such methods as reassurance and clarification of feelings gives teachers some means of structuring an interview.

The nondirective approach also has its limitations, however. It is time-consuming and circumlocutory. How much neater and easier it is to tell a student writer that he is in error, that there is a better way, and then proceed to the next item. Furthermore, although many aspects of writing are subjective, optional, and arbitrary (such as the foregoing selection of *furthermore* instead of *in addition*), there is a subject matter in composition about which there is no dispute, that can be taught directly, and that adolescents cannot readily improvise for themselves. This body of knowledge ranges from spelling and punctuation through aspects of usage, diction, syntax, and organization. And from the point of view of behavioral conditioning, nondirective techniques may fail to reinforce desired responses because of the tendency to avoid value judgments and to leave the client free to choose from an unlimited number of options in the course of helping himself. As in the case of most methodology questions, the issue is therefore which-when rather than either-or.

Looking at Mrs. L.'s recorded writing conference, one can see that she used some nondirective procedures to reach the student and to gain the girl's acceptance of suggestions and criticisms which were directive. Both the text of the transcript and questioning of the student gave evidence that she trusted her teacher and believed the experience to be valid and helpful. During the conference, Mrs. L. uttered many words of encouragement and praise. "You make some very good points." "You really know what you're reading." There were also instances of friendly disagreement, phrased felicitously. "Very true. But that would be another paragraph." "And you did back it up when you talked about the Thurber story. But then it seemed to me that you lost track of the idea." "Good, because that's really backing up your point. But that's what you've got to tell us."

Because the general tone of the conference was informative and useful and the relationship warm, the girl was able to weather even those few blasts that might have been avoided: "Now here's a case where you're being ir-relevant." "That's so awkward." The transcript, then, suggests that the teacher of writing can successfully combine directive and nondirective approaches during the composition interview.

Some secondary departments of English that appreciate the value of the writing conference require each teacher to see every one of his students at least once during the course of the school year. If most English teachers fol-lowed this rule, they would conduct 130-to-200 conferences; if conferences lasted no more than 10 minutes each, they would devote 22 to 33 hours to interviews, in addition to the hundreds of hours expended in correcting papers. Such a program is expensive in time and money; in districts that give teachers of English released schedules of time for conferences, there is a need to assure taxpayers and trustees that the costs are justified by both the theoretical value of conferences and by practice.

How can the English profession and school officials assure the public that teachers are spending the released time purposefully and fruitfully? The answer must be in conscientious self-direction by teachers trained in conference techniques and in supervision that encourages the best practices and discourages misuse or disuse of the conference. Highly competent supervisors of English can be expected to teach and demonstrate interview methods, observe conferences, hear tapes, and study conference records (Fig. 4) in order to suggest professional improvement.

SUPERVISING THE CONFERENCE PROGRAM

Because not many teachers abuse their relationships with children during the interview and because none is overly fond of supervision, one can expect some to resist when given direction in handling conferences. However, supervision is important because a few teachers misuse the conference to emphasize matters other than writing. They may be more interested in amateur psychological therapy for troubled youngsters; they may try to indoctrinate a world view that will give a questing adolescent purpose and commitment. Some misuse of the interview stems occasionally from impatience with the slow and immeasurable pace of writing growth; it may even be caused by a teacher's lack of confidence either in writing as a valid aspect of the English curriculum or in his own knowledge of composition. Whatever the reason, supervision and professional ethics must prevent the short-changing of students, for whom the conference may be the prime agency of motivation to write and to learn how to write better.

In a well-supervised secondary department of English, the chairman asked his staff to express their opinions of an organized program of composition conferences which they had undertaken. Negatively, they found the keeping of conference records time-consuming, the arranging of meetings at the mutual convenience of teacher and pupil difficult, and the giving of time to conferences incursive upon other work, such as correcting papers and planning instruction. Positively, they noted that their students liked the attention they received in conferences; that conferences made them better acquainted with children; and that pupils worked harder at writing, when they knew that their efforts would be the topic of a conference. In other words, the writing conference is a major effort that pays off.

PROVOKING, STARTING, CONTINUING, AND FINISHING

V

As important and as useful as the composition conference is, its direction is essentially towards the product and not the process of writing. In a previous chapter, reference was made to talk-writing as a means of focusing on the act itself. To explore the process further, one must ask what actually happens before the young writer hands his paper to his teacher for correction.

Frequently, the scenario reads somewhat like this: 1) The writer postpones action as long as possible, as he would a tooth extraction. 2) He may jot down an inventory or outline. Quite often, he begins to write his first sentence and then feels lucky if he can complete it. 3) After discarding several false starts, he may find that words, sentences, and even paragraphs are beginning to form. 4) The stream dribbles and dries up, maybe renewing its flow after much frustration. 5) The writer quits, hoping that his teacher will be absent on the due date, or the stream runs its course. 6) At this point, many students believe that the assignment is done and good riddance; some call on parental or sibling editorial review; a few know how to edit and polish. Such a scenario is commonly tragic.

MOTIVATING WRITING

Aware of the struggles and frustrations of novice writers, English teachers seek ways to help boys and girls through the arid moments and blind alleys that are the usual consequences of classroom-writing assignments. The eternal question is: how? How can we provoke a composition? Once begun, how to continue until completion? And, finally, how to energize an effort to submit a presentable and refined work product? Although many more are needed, there are some answers.

At one time few expressed open hostility to the chore of writing. Before World War II, the young Americans who went to secondary school were the more academic members of their generation and slated for college. With their parents, they accepted the ideas of respecting authority and taking direction from teachers, who they believed knew what they were doing. When teachers gave assignments, students carried them out or, if they did not, felt guilty.

When teachers assigned the writing of a composition, youngsters wrote, even though many did so not with excitement but with a conviction that what is unpalatable is hygienic—like cod liver oil.

Since then, things have changed. Most youngsters go on to high school, with the result that their teachers encounter many whose families have no special deference for the opinions of teachers, especially regarding the processes needed to rise socially and economically. White and black youth movements have further blurred the image of the teacher as the authority and expert who is to be followed without question. After all, teachers are adults and members of the Establishment.

Consequently, teachers no longer can assume that, once they have given an assignment, they may expect total compliance without any further ado. This is especially true of a writing task, because composing is difficult. Adapting to new circumstances, the teacher now concerns himself with ways of motivating writing. Even the titles of professional journals' articles reflect this necessity: "One Way to Stimulate Thoughtful Writing," "Creative Writing Must Be Motivated," "This Worked with a Low-Ability Group," "Motivation by Adopting a Ship." The man or woman who could devise a reliable method of getting boys and girls to write would become the darling of 100,000 teachers of English. Oh, for a pied piper like Marshall McLuhan to sell writing rather than to inhibit it!

Unfortunately, no one yet has discovered a solution guaranteed to transform young cynics into enthusiasts. But colleagues and supervisors know many English teachers for whom students are willing to write. This is more often an outcome of personality than technique and therefore does not lend itself to analysis and emulation. Nevertheless, there are some clues about the prerequisites for stimulating writing that recur in the folklore of the profession and in the experiences of seasoned craftsmen. Boys and girls seem disposed to work at writing chores assigned by teachers who themselves like to write, who know writing, and who feel comfortable when teaching the kinds of writing that students are expected to practice.

To teach youngsters to write it is not enough for a teacher to admire literature and to be familiar with criticism. Even the English major who is trained in research, in *explication de texte*, or in literary history is unprepared to teach writing, if he has little first-hand acquaintance with the difficulties a beginner encounters in drafting a friendly letter, a business message, a personal essay, a poem, a short story, an editorial, or even an announcement. For this reason, too many students undergo repeated exposures to book reports and rarely to the other forms of discourse. Having to write routinely or for a teacher whose heart is not in the assignment is quite sufficient to cause a student to abandon the field before the contest.

The enthusiastic and knowledgeable teacher can make writing infectious, particularly if he acquires the knack for devising composition topics of interest to a variety of young people in his classroom. One frequently used resource is the literature that forms the core of most English curricula. Adolescents can plunge eagerly into a play like Robert E. Sherwood's *Abe Lincoln in Illinois* because they are entertained by his portrayal of Lincoln as a wry humorist; they can sympathize with a young man beset by a haunting sense of failure; there is romantic appeal in Abe's encounters with the doomed Ann Rutledge.

By the time youthful readers arrive at the scene where Mary Todd reveals her intention to make Lincoln her husband, they are personally caught up in his fate and in the suspense that builds when Mary invites Abe to sit next to her on her couch. Sherwood ends this scene abruptly. Next he depicts Abe trying to find a way to retract his promise of marriage. At this point, the teacher can ask students to guess what Mary and Abe said on the couch. How did Mary get him to propose? Or did she propose to him? Since she had once mentioned the affection of Ninian Edwards's children for Abe, did she perhaps ask him if he hoped to have children of his own some day? Did he then, sensing her purpose, try to change the subject? If so, how? By telling a funny story? By asking her where she had bought her hat? How could she steer the conversation back on course without frightening him off? What could she say to emphasize her desirability as a wife? Would he assert his unworthiness as a husband? Would he cite his ungainly looks, his failures at jobs? How could Mary smooth over these attempts to wriggle free? Once the alternatives are clear, the teacher can then ask his students to write their own versions of the missing scene.

Besides motivating the writing of new scenes for plays or new endings for stories, literature provides models that students can imitate. The result can be serious, an attempt to compose a poem like Emily Dickinson's "I Like to See It Lap the Miles," which is constructed upon an extended metaphor comparing a train to a horse. It can be witty, a parody of a work, poking fun at the original, as does Charles L. Edson's "Ravin's of Piute Poet Poe," which contains such lines as "I was burning limber lumber in my chamber that December, and it left an amber ember."[1]

One of the problems of writing after models, however, is that few young people can compose easily in a style that generally takes an established author decades to perfect. Another arises from the fact that some literary styles are outmoded. To model sentences on the following, a youth must make a precipitous leap into an unfamiliar age and culture: "She mingled not in the festal dances at Vaucouleurs which celebrated in rapture the redemption of France."[2] Few writers today use the word order of *mingled not* and such words as *festal*. Teachers therefore must select models carefully for their ability to move rather than stall youngsters, when they set out to write. Although successful examples by students are probably the best models for motivating their contemporaries to emulation, not many are available in print yet; for this reason teachers must have recourse to contemporary professional models, which are abundant.

Literature also can provide the impetus for expository and critical writing, as occurred in the case of Mrs. L.'s assignments in the previous chapter. Other

---

[1] Quoted in Adolph Gillis and William R. Benet, *Poems for Modern Youth* (Cambridge, Massachusetts: Houghton Mifflin Company, 1938), pp. 172–174.

[2] Thomas de Quincy, "Joan and David," quoted in Francis Connolly, *A Rhetoric Case Book* (New York: Harcourt Brace Jovanovich, Inc., 1953), pp. 162–163.

examples include book reports, about which I have cautioned already, and research pieces on the lives and works of authors. Also, literary, psychological, and political issues in literary works can serve as writing topics. Why did Hamlet delay avenging his father's murder? Was Madame DeFarge justified in her ruthlessness towards aristocrats? Explain the allegory in Orwell's *Animal Farm*. Of course, teachers need to avoid subjecting pupils to a single form of discourse; if the search for mythic and symbolic elements becomes labored and precious, interest dies rather than is born. An overly mechanical or zealous association of reading with writing can nullify interest in both language arts.

The rapid growth in recent years of linguistics has led to demands that the teaching of language be accorded equal time with literature in the English curriculum. Proponents also suggest that linguistic studies should serve as the springboards for composition. If the teacher can work up a student's enthusiasm for sentence patterns or for transformations, there may be a carry-over into writing. A lively unit in semantics may find boys and girls eager to submit themes on how loaded words are exploited in public controversy. Youngsters may also enjoy describing and comparing regional dialects encountered during vacation travels. Abler pupils may be attracted to the challenge of rewriting an English paragraph according to the rules of French syntax. ("It to them remained some money, with which they hoped themselves to save from the hunger after to have escaped from to the tempest" is a sample line from Voltaire's *Candide*.) Yet one cannot entirely stifle a small voice which reminds him of how technical, abstract, and even mathematical much of linguistics is. The science of language may not appeal to reluctant writers any more than the science of immunology fascinates the child who has to submit to a booster shot.

Is there anything else for the teacher who finds that literary or linguistic subject matter cannot always help to motivate writing? Perhaps a wide choice of topics that relate to adolescent interests directly. Such matters concern boy-girl, peer, and family relationships, life at school, films, television, music, and current events, particularly as they relate to the youth culture and as they range from the breezy (clothing and hair styles) to the serious (poverty, race relations, war, school governance). Much of the writing about such topics is, of course, immature and rather dull reading for veteran teachers, who should not permit their adult interests and beliefs to detract from the realization that it is the only writing that excites certain pupils.

Of the various forms of writing, poetry recently has come to occupy a special place in the youth culture and is therefore a ready source of interest, motivation, and practice for writing in schools and colleges. Since the nineteenth century Romantics, as a medium of intimate expression, poetry holds many possibilities for untrammeled frolicking with language and boldness of statement, characteristics appealing to the young. These attributes of poetry, coupled with youth's concern today for protest, explain somewhat a current increase of politically and socially critical verse among students.

A poetic subject that predominates is a revulsion against war. The

handling of much of this writing is indeed fervent and sincere but also plati-
tudinous and weak in linguistic resources, as demonstrated by this typical
attempt:

A Prayer for Peace

by Larry

Oh Lord above us, in your own way,
We ask for the words to use today;
We are bound for a rally seeking Peace;
Give us the strength to keep our cools,
To be steadfast but not uptight;
We seek to abandon a Satan war, and
After this day we'll have war no more;
Give us this day the words to bare,
So that our Congress might finally hear;
A silent majority speak,
This is our nation's fourth biggest war, and
      for us war's reached it's peak;
Thank you Heavenly Father for hearing our plea;
An attempt to bring our soldiers home free;
This is our chance to twist Fate,
To show our world the difference between love and hate.[3]

If a student cannot avoid commonplaces in writing about war, he may
still entertain himself and his reader by imitating E. E. Cummings in rebelling
against punctuation and capitals as follows:

Which War

by Ed

dear god america i
   so want to
   salute your head
   but my arm's been shot off and
dear god america i
   want to stand
   with those who love you
   but you've shot up both
      of my legs and
dear god america i
   want to sing
   in praise of your way
   but you've cutout my tongue
dear god america i
   want to think
   now of freedom
   but you've shot me dead[4]

Occasionally dissatisfaction with war and society enables a student to
experiment with powerful, absurd metaphors and allusions, in addition to
departures from manuscript conventions:

[4]*Loc. cit.*
[3]*Vignette*, Nassau Community College, Garden City, New York, May 5, 1971, p. 19.

a virgin chick
in her sacred veil
stands on the corner
awaiting the sale
the mormon monk
preaches lemonade
my feelings sunk to my strict brigade
    ah, but you're all—
    you're all chained to the wall
    you're very small
    you're nothing at all[5]

Other than war, pollution also is a popular subject. Here, too, the easiest way is the cliche and the received opinion, especially by junior high students, as in "Pollution," by Brian, grade eight:

As I walked through the city smoke
    I saw millions of people starting to choke.
I could not get away; it was all around me,
    On my hair, on my clothes—I could hardly see.
I looked up above at the smoke-stacks so high
    And a cloud of black dust hit me right in the eye.
Wise up, all people, I'm telling you to;
    You must stop pollution before it gets you.

Loneliness and the disillusionment of finding weaknesses in adults, particularly parents, is another popular theme. Wendy, grade eight, uses a tone of irony in handling this subject in an untitled poem:

The baby at two years old,
With short curls, all of gold,
Lay in her crib, crying.
She was lonely.

The girl at fourteen years
Shed many silent tears
While she was crying
She was lonely.

The apathetic mother, always on the go,
Was too busy for her daughter, didn't know
That she was lonely.

The girl at twenty-eight
Announced her wedding date.
And her mother cried.
She was lonely.

In taking advantage of the built-in motivation to write poetry, the teacher must of course avoid discouraging young writers with negative criticism. Instead of remarking about the triteness of a cliche, one should commend original achievements, however modest, and also provide learners with good examples, by peers, to follow. On the other hand, excessive praise of

[5]Vignette, "Notch on My Barrel," David, p. 19.

uninspired or unconsidered work also is undesirable. Although generous in intent, there is an inclination among some adults, particularly reformers of education whose professions do not require them to toil in schools with any regularity or responsibility, to proclaim genius in the versification effort of a student, no matter how casual or derivative. Others heap praise upon any verse that is "relevant" or politically "correct," no matter how inartistically conceived. The learner thus is denied the perception that literature can be many other things besides protest. It also tends to obscure the fact that human fate transcends the ephemeral politics of the day.

In addition to encouraging students to compose poems about the cares of youth, the teacher can help them to broaden their range of enjoyment in playing with poetic forms, such as rhyme, meter, and certain miscellaneous devices.

Some observant teachers prefer not to stress rhyme because many youngsters tend to weaken their poems by forcing rhymes at the expense of meaning and of fun, as in "Rain," by Kathy, grade seven:

I hate rain
Because it's such a pain.
It is always wet,
And it affects my pet.
It waters the plants,
But it drowns the ants.
Sometimes when it rains, it lightnings,
And that can be very fright'ning.
I wish my brother would also go drown in the rain,
For he is the biggest pain.

Nevertheless, patience and practice may result in a model that suggests the enjoyment of rhyme without forcing, as in the case of "Afternoon," by Linda, grade seven:

Afternoon is mostly sunny,
You feel happy and funny.
You're free of troubles,
You jump the puddles.
The beach you comb,
Then walk on home.

When he uses rhyme unobtrusively and his imagination leaps freely and naturally, a student's poem can be an unexpected joy. Here is "Alone in My Room," by Debbie, grade seven:

When I'm alone in my room
I am peaceful and calm
And no one in the world
Can do me harm.
When I'm alone in my room
I have more than just fun,
I can be anyplace, I can be anyone.
I'm a witch, I'm a nurse,

> Or I'm even a queen.
> My room is a place where
> I let off my steam.
> When I'm alone in my room
> I can sing, I can dance,
> I can be in Australia
> Or else be in France.
> I can be at a party
> Where I'm throwing confetti . . .
> Then all of a sudden I hear,
> "Dinner is ready!"

Once in a while the rhyme is so funny that the reader fails to notice where it is forced. This is "I'm Feeling Kind of Sad," by Nancy, grade eight:

> I'm feeling kind of sad today.
> My Mom was drowned in Hudson Bay.
> My Granny was stabbed in the back,
> Then dumped into a burlap sack.
> My father was thrown into jail;
> We have no money for his bail.
> My brother took an awful spill
> When he tumbled down Owen Hill.
> My sister was just run over
> By a garbage truck from Grover.
> Suddenly I wake with a scream . . .
> This day has been an awful dream.

Like games and puzzles, metrical devices require the young poet to compete with himself and with a form. Here is a "double dactyl" composed by Lauren, grade seven:

> Heckelty, peckelty
> Charlie Brown's Snoopy Dog
> Little white beagle pup
> Has a big nose.
> With a bowl on his head
> Characteristically
> Top of his doghouse he's
> Striking his pose.

The haiku, usually three lines of seventeen syllables, affords practice in concentrating on a careful selection of a few words and images for maximum effect, as in this piece by Debbie, grade eight:

> The sun has come out
> To enlighten our cruel earth
>   and the people as well.

Both to meet the formal requirements and to express social comment in this manner is to experience an exhilarating feeling of competence.

It also is possible to give vent to the students' urge for the incongruous by trying limericks, which prescribe a set meter and rhyme scheme. These are by Lori, grade eight:

There was once an old lady from Wose
Who couldn't fit into her clothes.
    She tried to lose weight
    To go out on a date
But instead gained ten pounds on her nose.

There was once an old lady from Cripe
Who had beautiful things in her pipe.
    One day when she lit it
    She liked it and bit it
But found that it wasn't quite ripe.

The metaphysical poets of the seventeenth century invented a form that is somewhat of an innovation in the writing classroom today. Called the concrete poem, it is one in which the words follow the shape of the subject. Debbie, an eighth grader, apparently had fun filling a bottle shape with the word *bottle*, showing water flowing from the bottle and forming *drop*, and including a splashful of the word *spill*. (Fig. 5). Seventh-grade Carla expressed a common feeling of children in her concrete poem entitled "Sister" with the word *mean* repeated to fill in the girl's hair, with the comment *sometimes nice* reiterated to block in the face. (Fig. 6).

Sometimes related to concrete poetry and to puns is a technique

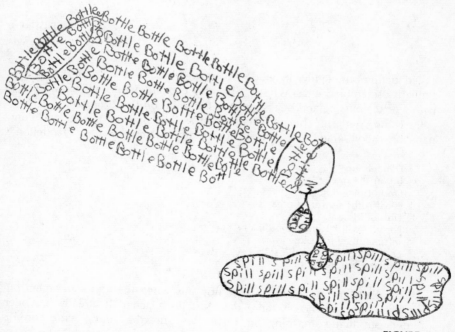

FIGURE 5
Concrete Poem by Debbie

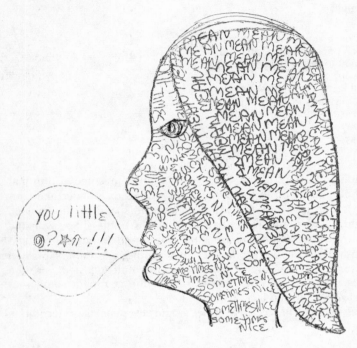

FIGURE 6
Concrete Poem by Carla

called *definitions.* Janey, in grade seven, defines mixed-up kid as *dki* and, similarly, scrambled eggs as *gseg.* She also explains world as *jigsaw puzzle with a peace missing* and buckshot as *dollar spent on the wrong thing.*

Some youngsters become very adept as they practice images and comparisons. Meryl, grade nine, offers a perceptive example in her "Dandelion."

> Dandelion
> If you see one,
> Do not pick it,
> For it is the flower of dreams.
> Do not blow it,
> For you will let loose the dreams.
> In time, they too blow away
> Leaving nothing but the stem
> Nothing but the truth.

Students are provoked to write not only when the topic stirs them but also when the audience is more than just the teacher. It already has been pointed out that composing for classmates puts the young writer on his mettle. In addition, to send a letter to another youth, to a public figure, or to a governmental or commercial agency is to endow writing with a purpose and an incentive which a classroom exercise cannot usually stimulate. To write in anticipation of seeing his words printed in a class journal or in schoolwide newspapers and literary magazines is a delight for the student who otherwise finds writing a bore.

Unfortunately, publications of writings by the young are not sufficiently abundant. However, there are some highly popular magazines that cater to older adolescents and often print readers' comments about youth culture, such as *Seventeen* magazine. Also there are some newspapers that feature columns of letters to the editor from junior and senior high school students. Occasionally, a book appears, such as the one recently distributed under the title *Anthology*. Containing poems by over 100 elementary children in the New York City metropolitan area, it was compiled by the Creativity Research Center of Fordham University. *Kids* is another monthly publication that features cartoons, verse, letters, and stories by boys and girls from ages five through 15. It is printed in Cambridge, Massachusetts. Beyond these, there are few opportunities for young people to be published. Here is an opportunity for a philanthropic foundation or for a state or regional council of teachers of English. Such an agency could underwrite the publication of a literary magazine that would be circulated widely and also would help teachers to provide an incentive for writing to those students who presently do not care to write.

Some advocates of creative writing believe that once the pupil begins to care, the rest occurs by itself; all that is needed is to get the student moving. Unfortunately, this does not always happen, because the creative fire can flicker out—after the first paragraph or even after the first sentence. When the first draft does reach completion, the needed editing effort may be lacking, because the young author has discovered that he has not satisfied his teacher's requirements. Motivation, then, is not nearly enough; the young writer needs to learn how to proceed and how to succeed.

For a student to compose an expository or an imaginative piece of writing, first and foremost he must have the desire to express an idea or an attitude, and he must also understand clearly how to solve those problems that will beset him, while he is putting words on paper. To help him, his teacher should plan classroom prevision activities that enable him to sustain his effort and to complete his undertaking. Previsionary lessons give specific guidance in charting the course of his intended theme, in preparing for future difficulties, in practicing and mastering the needed mechanical and rhetorical skills, and in recognizing when his product is adequate and finished.

PREVISION

Here is an example of how prevision works. English teacher Mrs. S. asks her ninth graders to write an entertaining essay about persons of their acquaintance. A member of the class, Bruce, enjoys the colorful personality of his milkman and decides to make him the subject of his composition. At Mrs. S.'s suggestion, Bruce makes an inventory of his materials, consisting of occasions when the man's actions were unexpected, incongruous, amusing, or particularly deft. He then writes some sentences relating one of these incidents, an occurrence during a delivery. Mrs. S. asks Bruce to read the words to the class; she has classmates tell him their impression of the milkman. If they respond as Bruce has planned, she tells him that the incident appears to merit further elaboration. (If it does not, then he should try another item in his inventory.) The teacher points out that reading words like *funny, hilarious,* and *silly*, which Bruce has used, is not as interesting as is reading quotations of the silly things a person actually says, descriptions of a funny appearance, or narration of laughable gestures and actions.

As a model of a description of a funny appearance, Mrs. S. reads him one from a Benchley or Leacock piece or from Irving's delineation of Ichabod Crane: "His head was small, and flat at the top, with huge ears, large green glassy eyes, and a long snipe nose, so that it looked like a weather-cock, perched upon his spindle neck, to tell which way the wind blew." Knowing how students tend to overstate caricature, the teacher cautions Bruce to avoid exaggerating the milkman's traits beyond the point of credibility. She also is aware that ninth graders have trouble with dialog and suggests that he practice a sheet of exercises in paragraphing, punctuating, and capitalizing words in a conversation. Having (hopefully) gained from the foregoing prevision experience, Bruce proceeds to write the first draft of his essay.

Although prevision, like steak, can be overdone, the tendency is rather to make it too rare, because it is arduous and time-consuming to plan and carry out. It is even more laborious, however, to correct and to bring about the revision of avoidable errors. The writer who is sent on his way with no more than a topic, unclear about procedure, and unsure of how his work will be received is likely to go astray. By the time he submits his paper, he probably has floundered too long and is too dispirited to start all over again, in response to substantive and numerous corrections. Having this happen successively he gives up, convinced that he cannot succeed as a writer.

FREQUENCY OF WRITING

While intended to improve writing, the trend of the early 1960s to increase its frequency militated against prevision. The Conant plan to reduce teaching loads in English called for a theme a week. Some zealots actually urged daily writing. Even in a weekly cycle, teachers found it difficult to create fresh and stimulating composition tasks for their students. In addition, the need to allot time for writing, correction, and revision left little or none for prevision. For some youths, writing became a treadmill that mechanically contrived themes to satisfy a schedule.

What frequency of writing is best suited to prevision? There is no doubt a minimum below which the novice writer cannot transfer learning from one act of composition to the next. This minimum has not yet been determined empirically for the various types and stages of writing. Until it has, a useful rule of thumb is to initiate some form of writing activity at least once every two or three weeks. Such a regimen leaves time for prevision and allows the teacher and the learner to concentrate upon the quality of the experience rather than its quantity.

QUANTITY OF WRITING

Wordage also has complicated the effort to balance quantity and quality. During the post-Sputnik years, there was much frantic assigning of long compositions in the 2,000-to-5,000 word class, as attempts at greater rigor. What resulted was a contest between English and other teachers for the homework time of students, who in turn competed with one another for available reference sources in school libraries and sometimes traveled long distances to find books that were unavailable locally. Often the students devoted greater efforts to taking notes than to composing.

After spending many hours reading hundreds of long papers, English teachers were forced to retrench. They decided to provide casebooks of articles and book passages as raw materials of research. Next they required fewer words, perhaps 1,000, and fewer sources for citation, reasoning that a student may learn to paraphrase, quote, and coordinate ideas just as well with a limited number of sources as with many.

Limiting the quantity of writing helps not only prevision but also editing, another essential step in the process of writing. When youngsters are not pressed to deliver a large number of words, and not speeding through one assignment cycle before beginning another, they have time to rework, to refine, and to amend their compositions. Junior high school teachers, in particular, find it important to allow such time during classes, because thirteen-year-olds generally lack the discipline and drive to push on through the succeeding stages of writing and editing; they may even be tempted to ask older relatives to do their writing. High school teachers of unacademic students and community college instructors of freshman English must also consider similar measures for young men and women who have not acquired editing habits.

EDITING

For both average and able students, editing is a major concern. Except for the unusually fluent and talented writer, poor writing precedes good writing, and editing is the only passage from one to the other. Many young people bog down at the first stage because of lack of interest and energy or habituation to instant success. Rather than persevere, they concede defeat and hand in papers that they know will earn low ratings. Teachers therefore are elected as trainers in the art of editing.

To assist a student in forging past the outline/inventory and first draft, one must provide a means for clarifying his thoughts, which he generally does not work out completely in his first trial. After his initial outpouring of impressions, uninterrupted by attention to technique, the moment arrives when the writer must ask himself some questions. Do these ideas make sense? Could I as a reader follow their logic and accept them as valid, if someone else wrote them? Is there a particular thought which I should consider more carefully? Does each sentence say what I mean?

Once he feels sure that his ideas are clear and sound, the writer must answer questions about placement and proportion. Does what I say here belong in this paragraph or elsewhere? Am I ambiguous in any way? What must I add to improve my reader's grasp of my meaning? On the other hand, are there any passages in which I have said too much? Are there more accurate words for any that I have used?

Teachers should also train the writer to manipulate his materials physically. As the student reviews each line of his draft, he should cross out words and insert new ones, circle phrases, clauses, and sentences, draw arrows to new positions, insert carets and paragraph symbols, and jot down marginal notes as reminders to check facts, to develop ideas, and to include new passages. He may also be encouraged to rewrite sections to be read aloud for comments by his teacher and classmates. Then he is ready for an improved draft.

Some English teachers prefer to have classes write the second draft quickly without any direct copying from the first.[6] The students themselves compare both drafts and then prepare a third, using the best elements of both previous attempts. Other teachers prefer that their pupils rewrite the edited draft, adding amendments as they compose again. Using a typewriter for the second draft is sometimes recommended as a means of changing pace and seeing one's copy in a fresh way. Whatever the method, the next step should be editing for spelling, punctuation, capitals, and usage. The last step is to compose and submit the final draft. After a lapse of some time, the teacher can, if he desires, require still another draft to help writers appreciate the fact that it is possible to refine writing even further. In addition, it will provide them with a concrete measure of their own progress in writing development.

The optimum number of editings and drafts depends on the student's capacity for rewriting. His teacher should strike a balance between what is sufficient in time and effort to edit and what is available in time and effort to supervise each stage of the process. As suggested previously with reference to peer-correction, having boys and girls serve one another as critics and editors helps such supervision. With experience, young writers learn how to perform a number of editing chores simultaneously, such as improving words along with mechanics, thereby reducing the burden of numerous drafts.

REVISION

When teachers correct papers, as many do, the classroom writing process should also, by rights, include appropriate revision by their students. This, however, does not always take place, suggesting a possible reason why teachers' corrections seem to have little effect on the way their clients write afterwards, the same errors repeating themselves. It may be that, when a teacher pays no further attention to a paper after correcting it, the writer devotes as little attention to red pencilings. After all, he may reason, if my teacher doesn't care, why should I?

To make correction count, the teacher must confirm what the student revises. There should be time for revision in class, supervised by the teacher,

---

[6]Mary G. Hamilton, *A Creative Approach to Writing* (Pleasantville, New York: Readers Digest Associates, undated).

who should later reread revised compositions to check on their adequacy. Otherwise, he wastes time initially correcting.

Supervising revision not only prompts the writer to take corrections seriously but also to avoid poor revision. A busy or careless pupil can overlook a correction in his haste. Or he may merely cross out a rejected item rather than exert himself to improve it. He may guess at the right spelling of a misspelled word, then proceed to misspell it in a new way, if he neglects to consult the dictionary. And even a most conscientious reviser can misinterpret a correction, misreading a word poorly written by the teacher or obscured by other corrections. He may also apply a suggested rule in the wrong place, or he may eliminate the entire statement when only a portion of it needs revision. Where peers correct one another's work, the teacher faces an added task, studying revisions to make certain that a writer has not gone along with mistaken advice.

The fewer students to be guided through editing and revision, the easier supervision is. With a large classroom enrollment, it is difficult for the teacher to keep track of each writer's individual place in the sequence of composition stages. One aid in keeping class records is the use of symbols to represent completed tasks, such as D1, D2, etc., for drafts, and R for a revised paper submitted in response to correction, or R1, R2, etc. to show that the first revision was inadequate and returned to the writer, etc.

HOW MUCH TIME FOR WRITING

Because students need motivation and prevision to get started, editing to continue and finish, and revision to benefit from correction, the teacher of writing must be generous with time. In the schedule that allots 40 or 45 minutes to a class period daily for English, at least three periods are needed for a writing cycle. During the first day, there should be motivation, prevision, and the writing of the inventory or outline. The second should be given to writing and editing. The third should take place after correction and be devoted to revision. If the wordage is larger than a few paragraphs, writing and editing may need two periods. If peers correct papers, add another period. The sum of periods in such a system is three or four every two or three weeks.

With the school year usually lasting 40 weeks or 180 days, a teacher who earmarks three days every two weeks for composition uses up about 60 days or a third of a year. Three days every *three* weeks reduces the time consumed to approximately 40 days or a little more than a fifth of a year. Adding another period in each cycle for peer-correction or for editing and teaching four periods of writing every two weeks, one totals 80 days yearly or almost a full semester. If his cycles occur only at three-week intervals, the total is approximately 50 days or about a quarter of the year. The range proposed here is from a fifth to a half a year. If one cannot teach writing as much as half the time in English, as recommended by James Conant, then he should spend no less than a fifth. Otherwise, he may not be able to motivate, prepare, and habituate writing adequately.

The advent of flexible scheduling may soon make the timing of writing instruction more appropriate to the task at hand. Where the stages of composition must now be expanded or compressed into forty-five minute packages, experience may lean towards a better distribution of minutes. No more than a half hour may be needed for prevision, depending on the class level. Writing and editing, which require more time and are usually rushed and interrupted by the bell, may develop best in an hour and a quarter or an hour and a half. It may turn out that peer-correction is best accomplished in an hour. With practice and supervision of writers, revision may not require more than a half hour. If the teacher wishes to duplicate excerpts from his students' papers in order to illustrate recurrent problems and solutions (e.g., run-ons, weak paragraphs), he may wish to use a half hour for taking stock or what might be called aftervision. A sufficiency of classroom time for writing may accomplish more than any single method once schools begin to schedule English flexibly, thereby enabling teachers and students to take the time they need to provoke, start, continue, and finish a cycle of writing.

GRAMMAR AND WRITING

VI

So, with the throttling hands of death at strife,
    Ground he at grammar;
Still, through the rattle, parts of speech were rife . . .
This man decided not to Live but Know.

Robert Browning wrote his "A Grammarian's Funeral"[1] in 1855 as a tribute to Renaissance scholars whose mastery of Greek and Latin had enabled them to revive the learning of the ancients. Thanks to these grammarians, Greek and Latin grammar and rhetoric were adopted as guides to literary style and rules for European languages by succeeding generations. In Browning's time and during the first half of the twentieth century, books of definitions of English parts of speech derived from elementary Latin grammar served as reference works for those readers aspiring to proper English. Classical grammar was similarly influential in the United States, where a young Abraham Lincoln walked several miles for a copy of Kirkham's grammar, which he used to overcome weak expression by memorizing definitions of parts of speech, relieving himself occasionally from these heavy matters with mathematical computations. Studying these definitions and parsing sentences continued as an important aspect of the language arts curriculum until the 1930s and 1940s, when child-centered educational philosophers began to challenge and question the tenets of conventional learning, among them grammar.

Stimulated by the writings of John Dewey and William Heard Kilpatrick, progressives in education decided that school children of elementary age were too immature to understand grammatical abstractions. Many elementary schools abandoned or deemphasized grammar and turned to creative expression in poems, stories, and plays. In districts where primary and intermediate levels jettisoned grammar and where high school English teachers felt that youngsters came to their level too late for effective grammar training, the junior high school grades became what are still widely regarded as the grammar years.

[1]Robert Browning, "A Grammarian's Funeral," *Poetry of the Victorian Period,* George Benjamin Woods and Jerome Hamilton Buckley, editors (New York: Scott, Foresman and Company, 1955), revised edition, pp. 237–239.

FUNCTIONAL GRAMMAR

As is the case of many educational trends, progressivist changes did not influence traditional grammar teaching in all junior high English classes; however, the attitude which prevailed in educational journals and in texts during the 1950s was expressed in the term functional grammar. Functionalism began largely as an attempt to limit grammar instruction to that which pupils were ready to learn. Because readiness was not always easy to ascertain, some teachers preferred to be guided by need. What students needed to learn was suggested by their errors in speaking and in writing. Analysis and tabulations of writing errors found the most frequent to be fragment and run-on sentences, lack of agreement between subjects and verbs, and poor placement of modifiers. (A few enthusiasts then told their pupils that any paper having a run-on sentence would automatically fail.) Thus did functionalism try to effect a compromise between child-centered and subject-centered philosophies.

Functionalism happily proceeded beyond the notion of eradicating errors. Although they endorsed criticisms aimed at traditional grammar, especially regarding the idea that grammar was a mental discipline, some teachers believed that aspects of grammar had direct and immediate usefulness in writing. They turned away from definitions and classification drills to materials that promoted the use of "lively" instead of "tired" adjectives and adverbs, precise instead of general nouns, and active instead of passive verbs. Such texts and workbooks also urged variety within sentences by shifting sentence parts from their usual order and variety between sentences by differing their types, simple, compound, and complex. Many grammar-composition schoolbooks advocate and drill these ideas today, and in some cases functionalism is found even within the same covers as ideas of linguistics.

DESCRIPTIVE LINGUISTICS

Structural or descriptive linguistics appeared dramatically on the grammar-teaching scene in the 1950s and began to fire salvos apparently heavy enough to sink a traditional grammar already awash from holes torn by progressives and functionalists. Before World War II, linguists had innocuously studied philology and the languages of primitive tribes. During the War, however, their knowledge became useful strategically. Later, during the boom in foreign language studies, educators became interested in linguists when it appeared that they knew ways of learning languages with unusual rapidity.

The linguistic approach was systematic and scientific: Obtain a "corpus" of language uttered by native speakers, usually through sound recording; isolate the phonemes or meaningful sounds by contrastive analysis, i.e., by making lists of words that differ in meaning and in one sound only (pat, bat); list these phonemes (p, b); analyze carefully how they are produced physically in speech (front labial plosive sounded or unsounded); identify their possible places of occurrence in words (initial, medial, or terminal); and give the learner drills in producing phonemes, words, and sentences. Using linguistic techniques of analyzing American English speech, Charles Carpenter Fries, George L. Trager, and Henry Lee Smith contributed much to the teaching of English as a second language.

As scientists, descriptive linguists objected to the old grammar as a body of learning based on unscientific and unverifiable conclusions, on definitions lacking in consistency and rigor, and on the prescription of forms unrelated to observable language behavior among American speakers of English. How can one account for the word *goodness*, they inquired, in a system that defines a noun as a person, place, or thing? It is more useful and precise to define a noun with respect to its structure; i.e., a noun is a word that can be inflected for two cases, the common and the possessive, and for two numbers, the singular and the plural. How can one accept such a subjective definition that a sentence is a complete thought? No wonder children are unable to write sentences. Rather, a sentence is an utterance with falling pitch and bounded by terminal junctures (pauses), one of a variety of strings of words arranged in specific ways—noun-verb, noun-verb-noun, and others. How can one insist that "It's me" is incorrect and that there is a distinction between *shall* and *will*, when recordings of educated speakers show "It's me" in wide use and *shall* and *will* spoken interchangeably? An immediate effect of this questioning was to shrink the number of usage items that English teachers felt obligated to correct.

Another effect of linguistics was to downgrade writing. Descriptivists made much of the fact that, historically, people always develop a spoken before a written language. They added that written language is no more than graphic symbols for sounds. As more teachers read and studied in the new field, one began to hear with increasing frequency that speaking was primary and writing secondary. Even though linguists like Sumner Ives objected, many popularizers and proselytizers hastened to the unwarranted conclusion that primary in chronology means primary in value. Consequently, many teachers of English believed that more time should be devoted to speech instruction than writing, while those who were neglecting writing felt that now they had a scientific-sounding rationale. This tendency gathered force until the post-Sputnik Conant movement rehabilitated writing and structural descriptive grammar lost ground to a still newer linguistics, transformational grammar.

Despite a negative effect on teaching writing, the structuralists made a positive contribution in the form of sentence patterns. As in the new mathematics, which was concerned with sets, the new grammar was full of references to structure and pattern. Definitions of parts of speech frequently used such expressions. Intensifiers pattern like *very*. Determiners pattern like *the*. Adverbs pattern like *often*. Sentences pattern like "I run," "He is tall," "He is a farmer," "They read newspapers." In this approach, teachers had students identify and practice writing various sentence patterns, sometimes in nonsense form to emphasize structure as opposed to meaning, which veterans of the "boing-boing" era can recall. Pattern drills made teachers and students aware of a large and reproducible collection of sentence orders available in the language; this kind of information was more specific and detailed than the few categories of sentences offered by the functionalists for achieving sentence variety.

Some structuralists proposed new ways of correcting fragment and run-on sentences. Once they had familiarized a student with the basic sentence patterns of English, about 10 in number, they proceeded to teach him to recognize a fragment as a group of words that did not fall into a known pattern. He could then correct it by remaking or expanding it into one of the basic types or by attaching it to one of them. (E.g., "after school," a fragment, can be appended to the noun-verb-object type, "I did homework," to make "I did homework after school.") By the same token, the structuralists taught run-ons as unconventional combinations of basic sentence types that would reveal themselves, when tested aloud for double cross (terminal) juncture signaled by a falling intonation pattern (dropping of the voice). When he detected such juncture, the student should insert appropriate punctuation, such as a semicolon or period.

Despite the predictions of boosters, structural grammar during the 1960s did not bury traditional grammar. Differences in nomenclature, although debated angrily, did not detract from a fundamental similarity between the two disciplines, a similarity that one linguist estimated at 95 percent.[2] It was noted that both persuasions used the same parts of speech and that much new was only different terminology for old. The old terms also persisted because English teachers were accustomed to them. In addition, the lay public continued to hold fast to a simple faith in the almost medicinal properties of the old grammar. Finally, much respect for the values of traditional grammar was restored by the ascendancy of transformational linguistics, a movement begun by Zellig Harris and Noam Chomsky and popularized by Paul Roberts. The latter abandoned the structuralist cause for the newer grammar, when he published *English Sentences* in 1962.

TRANSFORMATIONAL LINGUISTICS

The humanistically trained teacher of English who sees a work on transformational or generative theory, such as Chomsky's *Syntactic Structures*, may be needlessly alarmed by resemblances to algebraic or chemical equations. They merely turn out to be shorthand for parts of sentences and for rules of generating or producing sentences. (Hence the designation "generative grammar.") To transformationists, because structural grammar is concerned only with describing that which it hears, it fails to ask and to answer a fundamental question: how do people learn language? The transformationist answer is that they learn simple or kernel sentences first, and then later they acquire the ability to change the kernels into complicated sentences by applying certain rules of transformation. (Hence the term "transformational grammar.") Also, most children learn these rules unconsciously before they enter school and, con-

[2]Samuel R. Levin, "Comparing Traditional and Structural Grammar," *Readings in Applied English Linguistics*, Educational Division, Meredith Corporation, Harold B. Allen, Editor (New York: Appleton-Century-Crofts, second edition, 1964), p. 52.

trary to progressivists' belief regarding elementary-age unreadiness, should start early to acquire a systematic knowledge of English grammar.

Thus, a series of elementary texts by Paul Roberts teaches noun and verb phrases and agreement of subjects and verbs, in grade four, and adjectives, past tense, and the possessive "transform," in grade five. (A "transform" is a rule of transformation. In the case of the possessive transform, the rule is considered a series of four stages: first sentence, "Edgar has a horse."; second, "The horse is gentle."; transformation, substitute *Edgar's* for *the*; new sentence, "Edgar's horse is gentle.")

A measure of the transformationist swing back to tradition is Roberts's comments to teachers in the seventh-grade volume of his series. He says that its contents reflect a "rather formal" English, more suitable in writing than in speaking. "We are not interested in teaching the child how to chat with his comrades. This he can do without our assistance."[3] He observes that the grammar of the text generates forms used in writing, as in the case of the comparison transformation: I am tall. John is tall. John is tall $+$ er $+$ than $+$ I am tall. John is taller than I. Roberts adds that it is not necessary to tell a student that "John is taller than me" is wrong. One merely need not teach him how to generate it.

Other than restoring traditional prestige to writing, transformationism also is attempting to find an answer to the important question of maturity in writing. If we can determine what is seasoned writing, perhaps we can force-feed growth in writing. As long ago as Aristotle rhetoricians pointed to balanced and periodic sentences as the insignia of mature style. In the modern era, functionalists saw the true hallmark in the long and in the complex sentence. Generative grammarians take the position that mature writing uses more transformations than immature writing, especially those transformations of modification. To attain maturity of style students need practice in manipulating phrases, clauses, adjectivals, adverbials, and appositives. Consistent with the transformationist approach is that of Francis Christensen, of the University of Southern California, who claims to have found in samples of professional writing the kind of sentence that best exemplifies mature composition.[4] Rather than the complex sentence, it is the "cumulative" one, consisting of a main clause followed by clusters of sentence modifiers, which serve to invest the ideas of the main clause with density, variety in texture, and concreteness. In the sentence, "He shook his hands, a quick shake, fingers down, like a pianist," which Christensen quotes from Sinclair Lewis, the additive material contains a noun cluster, an absolute, and a prepositional phrase, all of which supplement the information in the main clause. Manipulating modifiers is undoubtedly a useful practice in the English classroom; it is moot, however, that the cumulative sentence is *the* key to better writing.

There seems to be no one key. Semanticists tell the teacher of English

---

[3]Paul Roberts, *The Roberts English Series; a Linguistics Program,* 7 (New York: Harcourt Brace Jovanovich, 1967), teachers' edition, p. T11.

[4]Francis Christensen, "A Generative Rhetoric of the Sentence," *Teaching English in Today's High Schools, Selected Readings,* Dwight L. Burton and John S. Simmons, editors (New York: Holt, Rinehart, & Winston, Inc., 1965), pp. 303–314.

that in the beginning was the word and that its connotations and levels of abstraction are the key. Grammarians claim that he who masters the English sentence is in command of the language. Others avow that the writer who learns to organize a paragraph can readily handle the logistics of a work of any length. The teacher also hears that each literary form, haiku or trilogy, skit or drama, report or dissertation, has its own technical requirements which the writer must experience. Recognizing the importance of the word, the sentence, the paragraph, and the full composition, the instructor essays to train his students in elements of style both large and small. He also tries to remember that technique is only half of writing and that content, ideas, and something worth saying are the yang of technique's yin.

In these difficult moments teachers of writing sometimes turn from the humanities to science, for solace. The next chapter reports what science has learned about writing through the medium of research.

RESEARCH IN TEACHING WRITING

VII

Few researchers have experimented scientifically with the teaching of English composition because writing is a subtle, complicated, and relatively unquantifiable phenomenon. As Shakespeare noted:

> The poet's eye, in a fine frenzy rolling,
> Doth glance from heaven to earth, from earth to heaven;
> And as imagination bodies forth
> The form of things unknown, the poet's pen
> Turns them to shapes, and gives to airy nothing
> A local habitation and a name.

It is difficult to count airy nothings.

RESEARCH IN THE 1950s

In tabulating instances of research conducted during the 1950s, reviewers commented that they could find very few examples in the field of composition.[1] However, during the following decade, there was a sharp increase, with the advent of new presidential administrations, new attitudes in Congress towards federal aid to education, and a new public impetus to make learning rigorous and scientific. Officials and educators called for research in English, particularly in writing. Some remarked that no one knew anything about writing growth because insufficient research had caused pedagogy to remain static since 1900. In response, the profession initiated Project English, a program which convened meetings of scholars at the Carnegie Institute of Technology, at the University of Illinois, and at New York University in order to draft goals and procedures for a national agenda of research in English. With dollars voted for Project English by Congress, an energized United States Office of Education funded research in colleges and universities. In consequence the 1960s were a decade of more research in writing than had ever happened previously. Unfortunately, it was still not enough.

[1]Herbert Espy, "Criticism and the Three R's," National Association of Secondary Principals *Bulletin,* 39 (September 1955), pp. 66–74; Arno Jewett, *English Language Arts in American High Schools,* U.S. Office of Education Bulletin No. 13 (Washington: Government Printing Office, 1958), pp. 34–37; John J. DeBoer, "Composition, Handwriting, and Spelling," *Review of Educational Research,* 31 (April 1961), pp. 161–172.

To obtain a crude measure of the quantity of research in writing and other language arts, one may count entries in bibliographies of research, hoping that such listings are relatively inclusive. The present author tallied 112 original studies (as opposed to reviews of studies) in oral language, 107 in composition, and 700 in literature and reading that Nathan S. Blount enumerated in each issue of *Research in the Teaching of English,* volume 1, number 1, through volume 3, number 2. All of these studies were conducted between January, 1966, and June, 1969, a period of two and a half years during which Project English was at its peak. It will be noted in these data that literature and reading experiments far outnumbered those in writing; yet, even in so prolific a field of studies as reading, controversies persist and theorists and practitioners debate methodology as in the case of phonics versus look-say, suggesting that hundreds of studies have not been sufficient to settle the issues. What can be said, then, about issues in teaching composition, where research studies number in the tens and not hundreds? Perhaps tens are not enough, either.

Another way of assessing quantity is to count investigations that relate to one another. Of the 107 composition studies listed by Blount, there are about 60 categories of seemingly related experiments. However, within each of these categories, not one study is a "replication" (research jargon for repetition) of any other. For example, of investigations in grammar and writing, three concern the effect on writing of structural grammar training, but each is unique with respect to procedures, content, or personnel. Of the few other clusters of researches, the following illustrate further the prevailing lack of replication: 1) peer-correction versus teacher-correction in grade nine and cooperative grading with college freshmen; 2) literary models in secondary school, children's literature and writing in grade five, and classics in literature and writing by British children; 3) oral drill and ninth-grade writing, oral drill and fourth-grade writing, tape recorders and writing, and oral-aural-visual stimuli and ninth-grade writing.

The rest of the titles in all categories are either barely related or unrelated. Among the latter are a study of what creative writing reveals about elementary children and another of what relationship there is between sixth-grade creative writing and reading comprehension. The unrelated topics are as mutually remote as an investigation of problems that fourth graders write about and a study of the quality of writing in third grade under conditions of varying time limits.

What is the explanation of little replication? Perhaps the fact that one usually makes just one original contribution to his field in order to earn a Ph.D. Perhaps another is the free-wheeling and democratic American way of allocating Project English funds instead of by means of centralized and purposeful direction, as in the Apollo lunar project. Whatever the explanation, it is almost impossible to draw conclusive inferences from research in writing without replication. The English teacher cannot be as sure that an experimenter's method will work in his class as can a medical doctor that the Sabin vaccine will work with his patients. Seeking confirmation of the value of prevision, for example, the teacher reads the report of a study in which the writing of tenth graders in a small city improved after prevision. If he is fortunate to encounter another study of prevision, it turns out to be one conducted with seventh graders in a rural community, and the prevision used is of another kind. If the results of several investigations under varying conditions are similar, his hopes for prevision may rise, but the results may not apply to his situation. If the results are different, as happens frequently, they merely serve to confuse him.

Because there is little, if any, coherence among experiments, it is difficult to find patterns of success or failure in methods of teaching writing. Prevision and other techniques must be tested repeatedly in a variety of school settings with uniform procedures and consistent results. Until then, teachers of writing will hesitate to view research findings as compelling or influential.

WEAKNESSES IN RESEARCH

The quality of research in writing, unhappily, is no more satisfying than its quantity. What is most deficient is measurement of change in writing ability, usually attempted by means of written essays or multiple-choice tests. Essays have the advantage of test validity; they are the products of authentic writing. However, because they must be judged by human beings, their results are usually unreliable. Readers who score essays independently rarely agree enough in their ratings to justify conclusive inferences. Multiple-choice tests, on the other hand, are objective and reliable, producing ratings that vary little. Their defect, however, is that they do not measure actual writing but rather skill in editing for errors of grammar, usage, and mechanics, an important but not a sole or even predominant aspect of composition, other components like style, imagination, originality, paragraph development, and organization being equally worthy of consideration. Although publishers of objective tests claim that their scores relate closely to students' English marks, such logic does not inspire confidence in those who question the ability of grade reporting to make fine scientific distinctions required in research.

The inability of essays and objective tests to gauge writing precisely is further compounded by time factors peculiar to education. Research studies of composition are generally limited to a semester or a school year because groups of students do not remain intact for longer periods of time. After subtracting days for beginning and ending a course of instruction, an investigator has no more than from four-to-nine months in which to apply experimental and control methods and to measure results. Because tests of writing are imprecise, they almost invariably fail to register appreciable change during four or nine months of learning.

This coarseness of instrumentation can be illustrated by some measurements that resulted during this author's research in peer-correction. As in the control group, the experimental classes registered an average gain of 3.7 score points in an objective test during a span of eight months. The standard deviation of the test scores at the end of the experiment was 10.0 points, meaning that about one-third of the students scored between 10.0 points below the average score and that equally as many rated between the average score and 10.0 points above. In other words, for two-thirds of the boys and girls, there was a range in scores of 20.0 points. When one compares a score variability of 20.0 with a gain of 3.7, he notes that average change detected by the test (3.7) was much less than differences that existed within the group (20.0). At the rate of change or growth of 3.7 points in eight months or about .46 points per month, it would take the students 43 months to grow as writers enough to equal the 20.0 range of variability within the group.

It has been pointed out, however, that groups in schools remain intact only long enough for four-to-nine months of measurement, during which time-periods the aforementioned test would be expected to register only between 1.84 and 4.14 points of average score gains. It is apparent that such a rate of gain is barely discernible within the time limits of the semester or school year. Tests that measure so little are hardly useful.

In other experiments with composition methods, researchers have found no gains, or they have even computed losses in average test scores, concluding that the teaching techniques studied have had no effect on writing. Such measurements suggest rather that the tests lack sophistication.

UNDERSTANDING STATISTICS

Another fact that teachers of English should know regarding writing tests is the meaning of statistically significant differences. Statistical computations can reveal the degree to which chance or accident explains differences between average test scores of groups of students. If a difference in average scores is such that it can occur by accident in fewer than five in a hundred tests, statisticians arbitrarily designate the difference as significant statistically. If the difference can happen by chance in fewer than one out of a hundred tests, the difference is called very significant statistically. Using these standards, a researcher can rule out differences that very probably occur by accident and thus can deal only with those caused by teaching methods and other educationally important factors.

A teacher should understand that statistically significant differences are not necessarily pedagogically significant. The 3.7 point test-score gain mentioned above happened to be significant statistically; that is, it probably did not occur by accident. However, it was not a helpful or a true indication of writing growth, as demonstrated. Studying a report that claims statistically significant differences, the teacher must be cautious about inferences that the experimental method makes for a genuine difference.

Even the lack of a statistically significant difference can be misleading. Where there is no difference of statistical significance one is inclined to say that different teaching methods apparently did not cause any difference in teaching results. However, a true difference in results can be obscured or balanced off by uncontrolled factors affecting writing achievement. In one study that compared the effects on writing of four-period as opposed to five-period English teaching loads, average test scores of experimental and control groups showed no significant difference statistically. Concluding from this finding that a four-period composition program was no better than a five-period procedure, a school board of trustees abolished the former. But some teachers with four periods had not conducted writing conferences with their students, although their loads had been reduced largely to provide such tutorial service. When no statistically significant difference was found, the result may have been caused by the absence of conferences. Had they been held, the difference might have been otherwise.

WHAT RESEARCH SAYS ABOUT WRITING

Given the prescientific nature of writing measurement to date, the English teacher cannot go to the professional literature of research expecting to find positive and exact answers to his questions. He therefore comes away with tentative information, such as: writing ability may relate to growing up in a middle-class family; it may or may not be associated with high intelligence; and girls are generally abler writers than boys.[2] He also learns that traditional grammar does not seem to accomplish much for composition, that structural grammar has helped in some cases and not in others, and that a transformational grammar experiment yielded mixed results.[3] In addition, the English teacher reads that intensive correction is no more effective than little correction or peer correction and that what appears adequate is frequent

[2]**Socioeconomic studies:** Walter D. Loban, *The Language of Elementary School Children*, Research Report No. 1 (Champaign, Illinois: NCTE, 1963); Jack McClellan, "Creative Writing Characteristics of Children," (University of Southern California, Los Angeles, unpublished doctoral dissertation, 1956). **Intelligence studies:** Irving Lorge and Lorraine P. Kruglov, "The Relationship between the Readability of Pupils' Compositions and Their Measured Intelligence," *Journal of Educational Research*, 43 (February 1950), pp. 467–474; Kaoru Yamamoto, "Threshold of Intelligence in Academic Achievement of Highly Creative Students," *Journal of Experimental Education*, 32 (Summer 1964), pp. 401–405. **Gender studies:** John C. Flanagan, "Implications of Project Talent for Research in the Teaching of English," *Needed Research in the Teaching of English*, Monograph No. 11, Erwin R. Steinberg, editor (Washington: Government Printing Office, 1963) pp. 80–97; William McColly and Robert Remstad, "Comparative Effectiveness of Composition Skills Learning Activities in the Secondary School," Cooperative Research Project No. 1528 (Madison: University of Wisconsin, 1963), p. 51.

[3]**Traditional grammar:** Richard Braddock, Richard Lloyd-Jones, and Lowell Schoer, *Research in Written Composition* (Champaign, Ill.: NCTE, 1963), pp. 37–38; Henry C. Meckel, "Research on Teaching Composition and Literature," *Handbook of Research on Teaching*, N. L. Gage, editor (Chicago: Rand McNally, 1963), pp. 974–982. **Structural grammar:** Jean McColley, "Effects of a Method of Teaching Sentence Structure upon Sentence Structure Used in Writing," Cooperative Research Project No. S-092, Kansas State College, Emporia, 1965, in "Research Abstracts," *Research in the Teaching of English*, (Spring 1967), pp. 95–97; Eva L. Klauser, "A Comparison of a Structural Approach and a Traditional Approach to the Teaching of Grammar in an Illinois Junior High School" (University of Colorado, Boulder, unpublished doctoral dissertation, 1964). **Transformational grammar:** Donald Bateman and Frank Zidonis, *The Effect of a Study of Transformational Grammar on the Writing of Ninth and Tenth Graders*, Research Report No. 6 (Champaign, Ill.: NCTE, 1966).

classroom teaching in which there is explanation, writing, discussion, and revision.[4] Research says little more than that.

Why then bother with research in composition, when it is tentative, inconclusive, and limited in scope? Maybe for the same reason that astrology had to precede astronomy. As in any scientific field, solid facts accumulate slowly at first. Writing knowledge presently is at the stage of intuition and mythology. Continuing research will eventually enter the domain of what is verifiable and, ultimately, precise and irrefutable. Meanwhile, there are more immediate returns from research—only for those who conduct it.

VALUES OF RESEARCHING

Designing and conducting an experiment can do much to sharpen the expertise of a teacher of writing, regardless of measured results. In planning his experiment, he must compose a statement of the problem he intends to solve or of the question he seeks to answer. He must also advance a hypothesis forecasting the results he expects and he must have a theory of how students learn to write that will explain the results. He also has to show a need for his study and how his research is a logical consequence of previous investigations. In so doing, he examines his own teaching behavior and his students' learning behavior afresh and objectively, questioning his previously unexamined assumptions and acquiring patience in delaying the making of inferences, until he tests his hypothesis. In sum, participating in research impels the teacher to rethink his ideas of what and how to teach writing.

How this process works is exemplified by a recent study of the relative merits of peer- and teacher-correction. During the year preceding the one devoted to formal research, a pilot study determined how teacher participants could give lessons that would reasonably distinguish a peer method from a traditional method without causing any harmful effects regarding human relations, learning, or management. During the trial and error period, teachers answered the following series of rigorous questions:

Traditional Method:

1. What should teachers' written criticisms stress? Should criticisms be encouraging or critical or both? Should criticisms be general, specific, or both? What should the role of correction symbols be? Should the teacher ever look for particular weaknesses?

2. How can assignments of compositions be made meaningful and, at the same time, uniform for research? Should both conventional and peer groups have the same composition topics? What should be done, if anything, for prevision?

---

[4]Lois V. Arnold and Dwight L. Burton, "Effects of Frequency and Intensity of Teacher Evaluation upon High School Students' Performance in Written Composition," Cooperative Research Project No. 1523 (Tallahassee: Florida State University, 1963); Joseph T. Sutton and Eliot D. Allen, "The Effect of Practice and Evaluation in Improvement in Written Composition," Cooperative Research Project No. 1993 (Deland, Fla.: Stetson University, 1964); William McColly and Robert Remstad, "Comparative Effectiveness of Composition Skills Learning Activities in the Secondary School."

3. Should students be required to revise all corrected papers? If yes, should they revise completely or only the offending parts?

4. What class discussions of papers should occur? What general composition instruction should occur? How can texts be used in this connection?

5. Should writing be done in class? If so, how much? Some or all? What kind of individual help should be given writers in class? Should they be required to write a revised draft before handing in a paper?

6. How should conferences be conducted? How can number and quality of conferences be made uniform?

7. Are the frequency of a composition every two weeks and a length of 150-200 words (present department policy) appropriate? If not, what is?

Peer Method:

1. Should students have a guide for criticizing each other's papers? If so, what should the guide say? Should peers ever look for particular weaknesses?

2. What is the best number of students for work in a subgroup, if criticism is to be conducted on this basis? Should membership in subgroups be temporary or permanent? On what basis should students be assigned to subgroups?

3. What should the teacher do during the prevision phase of the assignment? During the writing phase? During the correction phase?

4. After correction by peers, should the class be reconvened as a whole to discuss composition? What kind of general writing instruction should take place in class? How should texts be used?

5. Should students read their papers aloud to peers for criticism?

6. Should students write criticisms on original papers or on separate sheets?

7. Should a student read and correct a paper more than once?

8. Should students revise their compositions on the basis of peer criticisms? If yes, all or just the offending parts?

9. Since papers will not be corrected by teachers, how can grading be handled? How can conferences?

10. Same questions (2, 5, and 7), as under traditional method about assignments, writing, frequency, and length.

    While trying to find answers to the questions about the traditional method, the teachers noted that they were changing some of their classroom habits. One decided to consult the dictionary before correcting her students' spelling, after she had learned that she had been recommending wrong spellings. When uniform assignments were agreed to include a friendly letter, a personal essay, a narrative, and a description, and where a teacher who had previously been accustomed to assigning only book reports went through several topics with her classes, she commented, "I never knew there were so many different things I could ask the children to write about." With pupils writing a theme every two weeks without exception, teachers found that they had to reduce or delete other items from their curricula and that such frequency detracted somewhat from the spontaneity of writing. As a result, each felt that working in research had made him a more practiced and expert corrector and explicator of writing.

To answer questions about peer-method procedures, the teachers had to develop techniques without the aid of precedents, each day being one of discovery. In training students in correction, one teacher learned that they could not evaluate writing satisfactorily before much practice in revising their own papers. She also found it wise not to attempt peer-correction before providing guidance to entire classes, using duplicated compositions or sample writings made into projectuals and displayed during instruction. During peer correction, she also noticed that boys and girls were unable to direct the writers' attention to erroneous items without actually writing on the papers as teachers do, using the traditional method of correction. She solved this problem by having writers number each line of their compositions. Then critics could write separately, "See line seven for error in spelling."

In deciding to use guide sheets in answer to peer-method question number 1, a teacher noticed that her pupils were unenthusiastic about using the sheets she had devised but were eager to apply guide sheets composed by classes. A colleague noted that children were "surprised, pleased, and intrigued" by the opportunity to read one another's papers. At first skeptical about her students' capacity for correcting, another teacher reported that:

> Student's paper was read and discussed by person who rated it. I found myself in close agreement. After paper was discussed by rater, he asked class for opinions on attention-catching beginning and other points. Everyone seemed tremendously interested. It takes about ten minutes a paper, but, since each student is speaking extemporaneously before the group analyzing, judging, listening, etc., so many skills besides writing are involved that the time seems justified, at least so far.

Delighted by the comments that she overheard her students exchanging, a teacher kept a record of some of their remarks: "This conclusion is very unusual." "It's cute, but I don't think you give enough examples." "This doesn't make sense." "What did you do? Go over this thing with a magnifying glass? There's not one thing wrong." Another instructor learned something about himself: "You know, I always felt that my comments and corrections were indispensable. When I fell behind in my paperwork, I used to be stricken with feelings of guilt. Now I see that they can get along without me."

INTERPRETING RESEARCH FINDINGS

Teachers of English are too often needlessly reluctant to initiate controlled and rigorous experimentation. In addition, many hesitate to study research findings of others. Coming from training in the humanities, they are awed, discouraged, and sometimes repelled by the technical vocabulary of published research, which also uses mathematical tabulations, graphs, and statistical symbols of an apparently confusing nature. Yet only a smattering of the research lexicon is sufficient to decipher basic meanings, illustrated by an examination of a typical paragraph:

1) An analysis of the IQ data gathered for Group A, Experimental, and Group C, Control, shows the M of the Experimental Group to be 111.50 and that of the Control Group to be 105.23. 2) To determine the significance of the difference between the IQ M's of the Experimental and Control Groups, a t was calculated, using Fisher. 3) The obtained t was 1.83 and the interpolated .01 level was 2.700; the .05 level was 2.019. 4) Therefore, the conclusion was made to accept the null hypothesis that there was no significant statistical difference between the IQ mean of Group A, Experimental, and Group C, Control, since the observed value of 1.83 is less than the .01 level of 2.700 and .05 level of 2.019.[5]

Sentence (1) says that the M or mean (average) IQ test score in the experimental group (where a new variable in teaching was used) was 111.50, and, in the control group (used for comparison and using traditional teaching), the mean score was 105.23. Sentence (2) says that Miller used Ronald A. Fisher's formula called a t test, to find the effect of extraneous chance factors on the difference between these two mean scores, being $111.50 - 105.23 = 6.27$. Applying Fisher's equation to this difference (using a formula available in a statistics text), one obtains a number called a t ratio. He then consults a table of t ratios, locates a column that contains a figure equivalent to the number of students tested, and reads off t ratios for the .01 level (expected to occur by chance in no more than one in 100 cases) and for the .05 level (expected to occur by chance in no more than five out of 100 cases). In sentence (3), Miller states that the table she consulted read 2.700 for the .01 level of probability and 2.019 for the .05 level.

It will now be recalled that her application of Fisher's formula resulted in a t ratio of 1.83, which is less than 2.019. If, instead of 1.83 the t ratio had been as large as 2.019 or larger, the difference (6.27) between the groups' mean IQ scores could have been attributed to chance in fewer than five in 100 tests. However, this was not the case. The t ratio was lower, and Miller concluded in sentence (4) that there was no statistically significant difference between her experimental and control group in average of IQ scores, despite a mathematical difference of 6.27. This meant that the difference probably occurred by chance rather than by reason of a difference in intelligence between groups.

Such information is useful in findings of differences between groups in writing achievement or other skills after teaching, because such differences can be attributed to students' intelligence, not to their learning experiences, if groups can be shown to differ in intelligence. The reference in sentence (4) to null hypothesis is a way of saying that Miller hypothesized or guessed that there would be no statistically significant difference between mean scores. After the t test, she accepted or confirmed the truth of this guess. Had her t ratio been 2.019 or greater, she would have rejected the null hypothesis.

Understanding how investigators apply statistical techniques to test scores helps to allay the confusion that English teachers feel when they see research reports. As measurement in writing better detects composition growth, this knowledge will become more useful. Meanwhile it is not yet es-

[5] Dr. Frances Miller, English Consultant, South Central Educational Unit, "Sequential Patterns of Structures in the English Language Compatible with Written Expressions of Junior High Students," *Journal of Educational Research*, 59 (January 1966), p. 202.

sential for teachers to read statistical data expertly. More important are the investigator's theory, teaching procedures, conclusions, and recommendations read in a report of an experiment in teaching writing. His statement of theory presents his rationale about cause and effect in learning to write. A new theory can help the teacher to see his students and their written compositions in a fresh light or from a new standpoint. It also can challenge him to validate his own theories. If a research account presents a detailed teaching method (unfortunately, not enough do), he may uncover a model worthy and capable of emulation. Going directly to the experimenter's conclusions is one way to get to know his results immediately. Reading the section concerning proposals for future research, one may obtain the products of an investigator's careful and intelligent thought about the advantages, disadvantages, and implications for colleagues of what he has experienced and learned with great effort. Even if the researcher submits measurements that prove nothing scientifically and even if no statistically significant difference between compared groups is evident, his views about writing should be respected and studied, because he probably is a capable and ambitious teacher whose alertness and ingenuity have gifted him with perceptions of value to his colleagues.

SUMMARY

Research has not yet developed a level of quality or quantity to shape a useful body of information about how to learn and to teach writing. However, it should be encouraged in hope that eventually it may lead to definitive and conclusive results. Meanwhile, it is to the benefit of teachers of English to familiarize themselves with the language of research, in order to understand reports. They also may learn that conducting their own research is as exhilarating and rewarding as any other adventure that takes them beyond their present abilities.

AFTERWORD

The teacher of writing can accomplish his task with pride and satisfaction if his main objective is not talented writing but competent writing. Voluntarily to abandon writing would be to consign the next generation to a new Dark Age of incandescent bulbs. Although there is little reason to doubt that the difficulties of teaching writing have new aspects today, the observant teacher should be encouraged to note that what is noisiest is sometimes what is most transient. The mass media's interest already has begun to shift from McLuhan to other sensations. Despite an economic recession, which can be far more dangerous than "the boob tube," the publishing industry remains fairly solvent. With the opening of each academic year, young men and women who previously could consider only menial occupations are offered more opportunities for secondary and higher education and are in a position to acquire values of reading and writing. The business community still esteems and rewards competent written expression. In addition, writing still is essential to knowledge and imagination.

Having confidence in the uses and in the future of writing, the teacher of English can address himself to the problem of overcoming the inadequacies of traditional correction. A solution is available: to provide students with sufficient time to learn how to write by means of motivation, prevision, writing practice, editing, and revision in response to correction, supported and reinforced by the tutorial composition conference. He can supplement this basic approach with experimentation in alternatives to convention such as peer-correction, self-correction, and talk-writing, remaining alert to the even newer alternatives as they occur in professional literature.

If we must have a slogan let it be one that will vie with another catch phrase: Write on!

BIBLIOGRAPHY

ARNOLD, LOIS V. and DWIGHT L. BURTON, "Effects of Frequency of Writing and Intensity of Teacher Evaluation upon High School Students' Performance in Written Composition," unpublished Cooperative Research Project No. 1523, Florida State University, 1963. Report of a carefully administered experiment that discovered no significant differences resulting from varying amounts of correction.

BATEMAN, DONALD and FRANK ZIDONIS, *The Effect of a Study of Transformational Grammar in the Writing of Ninth and Tenth Graders*, Research Report No. 6. Champaign, Illinois: National Council of Teachers of English, 1966. Ninth and tenth graders at the Ohio State University School who studied generative grammar seemed to produce more "well-formed" sentences than the control group, but there were no significant differences in sentence complexity; although experimental group had more error reductions, other data were contradictory and inconclusive. Some would use these results to refute the idea that grammar has no effect on writing.

BLUESTONE, GEORGE, *Novels into Film*. Berkeley: University of California Press, 1961. Explanation of how writers transform novels into screenplays; good commentaries on filming of famous novels like *Grapes of Wrath*.

BRADDOCK, RICHARD, RICHARD LLOYD-JONES and LOWELL SCHOER, *Research in Written Composition*. Champaign: NCTE (1963). Review of composition research with useful guidelines for research designs.

BUXTON, EARL W., "An Experiment to Test the Effects of Writing Frequency and Guided Practice upon Students' Skill in Written Expression." Unpublished Ph.D. dissertation, Stanford University, 1958. Cited by Braddock *et al.* as one of a few well-designed experiments known in writing.

CHRISTENSEN, FRANCIS, "A Generative Rhetoric of the Sentence," in *Teaching English in Today's High Schools*, Dwight L. Burton and John S. Simmons, eds. New York: Holt, Rinehart, and Winston, Inc., 1965, 303–314. Advocating the art of writing the cumulative sentence in freshman English classes.

CLEGG, A. B., ed., *The Excitement of Writing*. London: Chatto and Windus, Limited, 1964. Tries to persuade British teachers to abandon the drill and test approach in favor of enjoyment of language through personal writing; has samples of compositions from secondary schools and commentaries about practice and correction.

CONANT, JAMES B., *The American High School Today*. New York: McGraw-Hill Book Company, 1959. Recommendations to enable American education to compete intellectually in the post-Sputnik era; influential for a time in advocating the four-period English load to upgrade writing.

CORBIN, RICHARD, *The Teaching of Writing in Our Schools*. New York: Macmillan Company, 1966. Essentially for parents and the general public but also useful for teachers; explains objectives and problems of teaching writing in American schools and tells why and how writing is evaluated by teachers.

DUSEL, WILLIAM J., "Determining an Efficient Teaching Load in English," *Illinois English Bulletin*, 43 (October 1955), 1–19. Account of the study that was most influential in the movement to reduce English teaching loads.

EVANS, WILLIAM H. and JERRY L. WALKER, *New Trends in the Teaching of English in Secondary Schools*. Chicago: Rand McNally Co., 1966. Has a short chapter on writing with general references to research, "prewriting," correction, and literary models.

FELLOWS, JOHN E., *The Influence of Theme-Reading and Theme-Correction on Eliminating Technical Errors in the Written Compositions of Ninth-Grade Pupils*, Studies in Education, VII. Iowa City: University of Iowa, 1932. Early experiment in correction using error counts as measurement; found correction no more effective than no correction.

GODSHALK, FRED I., FRANCES SWINEFORD, and WILLIAM E. COFFMAN, *The Measurement of Writing Ability*. New York: College Entrance Examination Board, 1966. On an attempt to construct an instrument for valid mass testing of composition; concludes that best measurements came from combination of essay or "interlinear" tests with objective writing and verbal aptitude tests; resolves problem of differences among raters by summing their ratings, a moot procedure.

GRADY, MICHAEL, "A Technique for Theme Correction," in *Classroom Practices in Teaching English: a Fifth Report of the NCTE Committee on Promising Practices*, 77–81. Champaign: NCTE, 1967. On having college students correct their own writings, Grady feels that it helps student writers to learn objectivity, encourages desire to avoid errors, motivates desire to confer with instructor, and helps justify report-card grade; weaknesses include tendency of students to undergrade themselves and to miss subtle errors of logic and agreement.

HAWAII DEPARTMENT OF EDUCATION, *Comparison of the Lay Reader Treatment with Other Treatments in Increasing Student Growth in Writing, 1968–1969*, publication no. TAC 70–1852. *The Use of Two Types of Paraprofessionals in Promoting Student Growth in Writing, 1969–1970*, publication no. TAC 70–1853. *The Composition Study: Summaries of Comparison of the Lay Reader Treatment with Other Treatments in Increasing Student Growth in Writing, 1969–1970*, publication no. TAC 70–1854. Honolulu: Office of Library Services/TAC, 1970. Reports of two-year study conducted by Dr. Patsy Saiki in ten Oahu high schools, grades nine, ten, and twelve; found no significant statistical differences among control and experimental groups having lay readers, taped corrections, or reduced pupil loads for teachers, although all but reduced loads had effects; also noted that lay readers were useful in accelerating correction and increasing tutorial conferences, while educational assistants gave teachers more time to develop instruction. One of the most recent of several experiments hampered by unreliable raters and inadequate tools of measurement but nevertheless important because of careful preparation of writing instruction and rigorous examination of factors that influence writing.

KOCH, KENNETH, *Wishes, Lies, and Dreams; Teaching Children to Write Poetry*. New

York: Chelsea House Publishers, 1970. How a poet taught verse-writing to children in grades one through six; fine examples of poems about wishes, comparisons, dreams, imagination, and color; useful ideas for younger secondary pupils.

LEVIN, SAMUEL R., "Comparing Traditional and Structural Grammar," in *Readings in Applied English Linguistics*, second edition, Harold B. Allen, ed. 46–53. New York: Appleton-Century-Crofts, Educational Division, Meredith Corporation, 1964. Although structuralists define sentence elements by example in contrast to traditionalists' definition by generalization, they have much in common, according to Levin.

LOBAN, WALTER D., *The Language of Elementary School Children*, Research Report No. 1. Champaign: NCTE, 1963. Longitudinal study of language development between grades one and six, using generative "communication" units for measurement; suggests teaching pupils how to use variations of basic sentence patterns.

LONDON ASSOCIATION FOR THE TEACHING OF ENGLISH, *Assessing Compositions*. London: Blackie and Son, Limited, 1965. Samples of writings by British adolescents with incisive analysis by teachers.

MAIZE, RAY C., "Two Methods of Teaching English Composition to Retarded College Freshmen," *Journal of Educational Psychology*, 45 (January 1954), 22–28. One of the few studies of correction; found frequent writing and peer correction worked with college freshmen.

McCOLLY, WILLIAM and ROBERT REMSTAD, "Comparative Effectiveness of Composition Skills Learning Activities in the Secondary School," unpublished Cooperative Research Project No. 1528, University of Wisconsin, 1963. For grades 8–12 at Wisconsin High School, researchers concluded that writing cannot improve without instruction in composition. Surprisingly, they also found tutoring ineffective.

McLUHAN, MARSHALL, *Understanding Media; the Extensions of Man*. New York: McGraw-Hill, 1964. How and why electronic media are supposed to be replacing print; influential philosophically among young writers, English teachers, and publicists during the late 1960s.

—— and QUENTIN FIORE, *The Medium Is the Massage*. New York: Bantam Books, 1967. Short, illustrated, and playful version of *Understanding Media*.

MECKEL, HENRY C., "Research on Teaching Composition and Literature," in *Handbook of Research on Teaching*, N. L. Gage, ed., 974–982. Chicago: Rand McNally Co., 1963. Review of recent research, including a good summary of researches in the effect of grammar on writing.

PATTERSON, C. H., *Theories of Counseling and Psychotherapy*. New York: Harper and Row Publishers, Inc., 1966. Descriptions and balanced assessments of schools of psychology and guidance.

PEI, MARIO, *What's in a Word; Language—Yesterday, Today, and Tomorrow*. New York: Hawthorn Books, 1968. Lover of language refutes McLuhan.

ROBERTS, PAUL, *The Roberts English Series; a Linguistics Program*. New York: Harcourt Brace Jovanovich, Inc., 1967. Transformational grammar plus composition and literature text for grades seven through nine. Emphasis is on enjoying language as an intellectual exercise.

RUSSELL, DAVID H., "Higher Mental Processes," *Encyclopedia of Educational Research* (1960), third edition, 645–657. Review of research in thought, theories of thought, associative thinking, problem solving, critical thinking, creative thinking, and developing and improving thinking abilities; concludes that many thinking skills can be learned.

SMITH, DORA V., *Class Size in High School English*. Minneapolis: University of Minnesota Press, 1931. Dissertation about an experiment with large classes and peer-correction by a pioneer in pedagogy of English.

SQUIRE, JAMES R. and ROGER K. APPLETON, *High School English Instruction Today: the National Study of High School English Programs*. New York: Appleton-Century-Crofts, Educational Division, Meredith Corporation, 1968. Based on visits to a number of high schools, report deplores teaching of English with respect to teacher education, supervision of instruction, curriculum development, and teaching of composition, language, reading, and speech; finds that only literary study gets sufficient emphasis.

TAYLOR, THEODORE, *People Who Make Movies*. Garden City: Doubleday and Company, 1967. Job descriptions in the film industry.

U.S. Bureau of Labor Statistics, *Occupational Outlook Handbook*, Bulletin no. 1550. Washington, D.C.: Government Printing Office, 1968. Periodical forecast of labor-market needs with job descriptions.

ZIVELY, SHERRY, "A Cautious Approach to Student Grading," *English Journal*, 56 (December 1967), 1321–1322. Article about classes that tried peer-correction.

ZOELLNER, ROBERT, "Talk-Write: a Behavioral Pedagogy for Composition," *College English*, 30 (January 1969), 267–320. Iconoclastic, witty, stimulating, scientistic, and verbose essay aimed at revolutionizing writing pedagogy by means of operant conditioning techniques; must reading for anyone who believes in teaching writing.

INDEX